Making Risk Management

Making risk management work means engaging people to identify, own and manage risk. Many organisations have spent considerable time and money setting up risk frameworks, processes, and supporting tools, but these have failed to deliver value. Instead, they should focus on the people.

Bringing together the expertise of Ruth Murray-Webster in the human aspects of risk management and Penny Pullan's deep expertise in facilitation, creative collaboration, and virtual leadership, this book provides tried and tested approaches to make each process step work well within the context of your own organisation and serves as a guide as to how to work effectively with groups. By translating a highly technical and complex subject into an easy-to-follow guide, this book goes beyond 'tick-box' approaches and provides top tips on how to engage others in developing risk management solutions and how to avoid many of the common pitfalls. This new edition includes two brand new chapters, one taking a deeper dive into the common decision-biases among groups in organisations, and one looking at remote and hybrid ways of communication and facilitation.

If you are involved in trying to make risk management work, whatever the context, this book will provide you with support and practical advice, in an approachable way, supported by real-life examples and memorable illustrations.

Ruth Murray-Webster is a recognised leader of project-based organisational change and risk management, performing roles as a practitioner, advisor, facilitator, researcher, and author. She is passionate about helping people overcome the many pitfalls involved in making risk management work. See www.potentiality.uk.

Penny Pullan is a pioneer of virtual leadership, expert on effective workshops, and facilitator of creative collaboration. Penny has run countless risk workshops over the years: in person, remote and hybrid. Like Ruth, she has written a number of books! See www.makingprojectswork.co.uk.

"If you only want to read one book on risk, I thoroughly recommend this text, it is digestible, wise, and offers solid advice to anyone who wants to drive best practice risk thinking into their work, or into their business."

Dr Michelle Tilley, C.Dir., *Director, Hinkley Point C, for EDF Energy*

"The section on 'Potential Pitfalls and How to Overcome Them' in particular is a masterpiece of concision and common sense."

Nick De Voil, *Consultant and Author of User Experience Foundations*

Praise for the first edition: *A Short Guide to Facilitating Risk Management*

"Risk meetings don't have to be boring: *A Short Guide to Facilitating Risk Management* is the book that risk managers have been waiting for. It provides practical guidance on facilitating risk workshops and making risk management happen outside of the workshop setting as well. Dotted throughout with cartoons, the emphasis is on practical guidance for getting things done without suffocating those poor souls who have to attend risk reviews. The book provides a clear introduction to tackling risk (including opportunities) in a fun, professional way, with the aim of gaining consensus. It's pragmatic and practical, with real-life examples to show how risk management can become ingrained in the day-to-day management of initiatives in your organisation."

Elizabeth Harrin, *author of* Project Management in the Real World

Making Risk Management Work

Engaging People to Identify, Own and Manage Risk

Second edition

**Ruth Murray-Webster
and Penny Pullan**

Routledge
Taylor & Francis Group
LONDON AND NEW YORK

Cover image: Rachael Brind-Surch

Second edition published 2023
by Routledge
4 Park Square, Milton Park, Abingdon, Oxon, OX14 4RN

and by Routledge
605 Third Avenue, New York, NY 10158

Routledge is an imprint of the Taylor & Francis Group, an informa business

© 2023 Ruth Murray-Webster and Penny Pullan

The right of Ruth Murray-Webster and Penny Pullan to be identified as authors of this work has been asserted in accordance with sections 77 and 78 of the Copyright, Designs and Patents Act 1988.

All rights reserved. No part of this book may be reprinted or reproduced or utilised in any form or by any electronic, mechanical, or other means, now known or hereafter invented, including photocopying and recording, or in any information storage or retrieval system, without permission in writing from the publishers.

Trademark notice: Product or corporate names may be trademarks or registered trademarks, and are used only for identification and explanation without intent to infringe.

First edition published by Gower Publishing 2011 and Routledge 2016

British Library Cataloguing-in-Publication Data
A catalogue record for this book is available from the British Library

Library of Congress Cataloging-in-Publication Data
Names: Murray-Webster, Ruth, author. | Pullan, Penny, author.
Title: Making risk management work : engaging people to identify,
   own and manage risk / Ruth Murray-Webster and Penny Pullan.
Description: Second edition. | Milton Park, Abingdon, Oxon ; New York,
   NY : Routledge, 2023. | Includes bibliographical references and index.
Identifiers: LCCN 2022015167 (print) | LCCN 2022015168 (ebook) |
   ISBN 9781032158341 (hardback) | ISBN 9781032158358 (paperback) |
   ISBN 9781003245858 (ebook)
Subjects: LCSH: Risk management.
Classification: LCC HD61 .M86 2023 (print) | LCC HD61 (ebook) |
DDC 658.15/5—dc23/eng/20220407
LC record available at https://lccn.loc.gov/2022015167
LC ebook record available at https://lccn.loc.gov/2022015168

ISBN: 9781032158341 (hbk)
ISBN: 9781032158358 (pbk)
ISBN: 9781003245858 (ebk)

DOI: 10.4324/9781003245858

Typeset in Georgia
by Apex CoVantage, LLC

Contents

	About the authors	vi
	Foreword	viii
	Preface to the second edition	x
	Acknowledgements for the second edition	xi
1	Introduction	1
2	What is risk management?	6
3	Why people and their perceptions matter	31
4	Why risk facilitation matters	47
5	Facilitating the risk management process	65
6	Risk workshops	83
7	Making virtual risk management work, whether fully remote or hybrid	103
8	Potential pitfalls and how to overcome them	121
9	Ten golden guidelines for the risk facilitator	151
	Index	155

About the authors

Ruth Murray-Webster
Dr Ruth Murray-Webster is an experienced consultant and practitioner in the areas of organisational change and risk management.

Ruth has more than 30 years of experience in a series of roles to enable organisations in most sectors to deliver change objectives. Recent appointments include Director, Change Portfolio and Group Head of Risk for a major port operator and Director, Risk in the Boardroom practice for KPMG LLP. Ruth researched organisational change from the perspective of the recipients of change for an Executive Doctorate at Cranfield School of Management. She is Associate Fellow at the University of Oxford, Saïd Business School where she is an experienced programme director and learning facilitator, as well as teaching in her specialist areas of change leadership, risk, and complexity.

Ruth's interest in risk management arose from a passion to help organisations to take educated risks, not avoid them or resort to 'turning the risk handle' without adding value. She has co-authored four books on the people aspects of risk management with David Hillson (*Understanding and Managing Risk Attitude*, 2007; *Managing Group Risk Attitude*, 2008; *A Short Guide to Risk Appetite*, 2012; and *Making Risky and Important Decisions*, 2021). Her work with Eleanor Winton – *The Disruption Game Plan*, 2021 – brings together work on strategy, innovation, risk, and change (www.disruptiongameplan.com).

Ruth was awarded an Honorary Fellowship of the Association for Project Management in 2013 for her services to risk and change. The synergies between the two disciplines continue to drive Ruth's thinking, writing, and practice.

www.potentiality.uk
www.disruptiongameplan.com
www.making-decisions.com

Penny Pullan
Clients engage Dr Penny Pullan when they are grappling with the challenges of making things happen in our increasingly uncertain and complex world. Her specialism is virtual, hybrid, and in-person leadership through facilitation. This engages people to identify, own, and manage risk. Penny built her skills leading projects and programmes of change for multinational companies and now focuses on developing the competence and confidence of others leading risky change. Penny brings clarity, confidence, and powerful communication, making people more effective, projects more successful, and work much more fun for everyone. She is a keynote speaker, a consultant, and a facilitator, and she holds a number of certifications including a PhD from Cambridge and Master Facilitator from the International Association of Facilitators (IAF). The COVID-19 pandemic widened her client base to include doctors, educators, leaders in local and national government, and small businesses from around the world.

Penny's previous books include *Virtual Leadership: Practical Strategies for Success With Remote or Hybrid Work and Teams*, 2nd Ed (Kogan Page, 2022), *Making Workshops Work: Creative Collaboration for Our Time* (PIP, 2021), *Managing Successful Programmes*, 5th Ed, co-author (TSO, 2020), *Business Analysis and Leadership: Influencing Change*, co-editor (Kogan Page, 2013). She loves to hear from readers and point them in the right direction to develop their skills to thrive.

www.makingprojectswork.co.uk

Foreword

This simple but effective book is aimed at those of you who do not want, or do not have the time, to digest a risk bible, looking up a glossary of terms just to navigate your way through the complex language, and feel at the end of it that you gained nothing. This text is for those of you who recognise that risk is a fundamental underlying tenet of your role, business, projects, investments, and decision-making in any context, and who want to be able to think about risk in a simple and value-adding way as part of your day job.

In my experience as a senior infrastructure leader, understanding risk is really very important to the way I make decisions. Each one of us makes decisions every day based on feeling confident that we have assessed the risk, but we perhaps forget that assessing risks is also part of our everyday life. Crossing the road, choosing which ATM to use, driving our car, all risk-assessed actions, all of which require confident risk-based decisions.

In business, teams and individuals struggle to get the risk basics right, often over-complicating their models and processes and ultimately turning off their audience. Never has this felt more of an issue than now, in today's remote working business climate. The practice of effective risk management needs to be accessible to everyone, not just practiced by experts and done to everyone else.

For me, risk is the golden thread with which we mitigate our costs, understand our schedule, drive progress and accountability, and improve our outcomes, all of which inform and underpin confident business decisions at any level.

If you only want to read one book on risk, I thoroughly recommend this text, it is digestible, wise, and offers solid advice to anyone who wants to drive best practice risk thinking into their work or into their business.

Dr Michelle Tilley, C.Dir.
Director, Hinkley Point C, for EDF Energy

Preface to the second edition

When we wrote the first edition of this book, we wanted to provide support for people to develop the skills to engage others to identify, own, and manage risk successfully. Our experience of doing this was mainly within major companies. Little did we know that 10 years later risk assessment and risk management would be everyday words around the world for large companies, of course, but also for small businesses, community organisations, education settings, and even within families. Now our world seems to be even more uncertain, and in this context we offer this updated edition to help you make risk management work. We hope that you find it helpful, accessible, and above all, effective as you deal with the reality of life today.

Acknowledgements for the second edition

Every author has many people to thank genuinely, and on the second time round we have more than ever!

The list of people to thank for this book is extensive. This is because we used questions, stories, and insights from so many practitioners working with risk management in business. They've helped us shape the structure and content of what we have written, both in this book and on www.makingriskwork.com. We wanted the book to be *directly* relevant to readers, so we didn't want to assume what those readers might think. So, a big thank you to all those who contributed their thoughts. We can't name everyone individually because there are too many people, but you know who you are. We will, though, name three organisations who gave us the opportunity to meet groups of risk facilitators at special events: the Association for Project Management, the British Computer Society, and the International Institute for Business Analysis UK Chapter.

We are particularly grateful to four risk facilitators who have allowed us to share their stories in detail: Vivien, Chris, and Anna in Chapter 4, and Tony, along with his alien invaders, in Chapter 6. Thank you! We know you are doing a great job, and it has been good to share some of your success in this book.

Three other people have contributed their time and talents to make this book so much better than we could have created on our own.

First, Vanessa Randle, whose illustrations have brought the text to life for us, and hopefully for you too. Vanessa retains copyright of all her images we have used.

Second, Rachael Brind-Surch, who helped us with extra illustrations specifically for the second edition.

Third, Malcolm Pullan, who pored over every chapter, making the first edition much clearer as a result: removing jargon, rephrasing ideas, and giving us a different perspective.

Then there's the team at Gower and latterly Routledge: Jonathan Norman for seeing the potential for the title as part of the Short Guide series, Rebecca Marsh for the second edition, and the whole team for their support.

Our friend David Hillson is mentioned a number of times as his work has been such an influence on us both.

And finally, our families. They have encouraged us to keep going even when they'd rather have us all to themselves: through many a late-night editing session (Ruth) or writing chapters on holiday when it was too rainy to venture out (Penny). So, to end this long list of thanks, we dedicate this book, with our love, to Malcolm, Kathleen, and Richard Pullan and Fred, Josh, and Helen Murray-Webster.

1 Introduction

Achieving your objectives relies on making good decisions in risky and important situations. Many organisations have defined risk management processes to help them do this. Others just muddle along doing the occasional risk assessment as required. Often these approaches don't deliver value. Although almost always logically correct, formal risk management processes tend not to take into account the influence of people. This book is designed to help you achieve your objectives by working with and through people to identify, own, and manage risk.

Who is this book for?

This book is for all those who want to make sound decisions in important but risky situations: people who need to work with groups to identify, prioritise, and respond to risks, and who wish to deliver value.

Does this apply to you? Maybe you have one of these job titles?

- Operations manager
- Project or programme manager
- Business analyst
- Risk facilitator or manager

DOI: 10.4324/9781003245858-1

- Internal or external consultant
- Director
- Health and safety manager
- Human resources professional
- Parent, football coach, vicar, administrator, or . . . insert your job title!

In truth, your job title does not matter. The only thing that matters is that you are involved with a risk management process in some way. If you are, you're likely to plan and lead conversations, meetings, or workshops where risks are discussed. You probably also give advice to others and coordinate people. In short, your role is to get risk management to work through other people. Throughout this book, we will use the term 'risk facilitator' to describe people who carry out such tasks, irrespective of their official job title.

Are conversations, meetings, and workshops that focus on risk different? We believe they are, and that's why we've written this book. When people discuss risk, they are trying to predict the future in a way that is as rational as possible, yet we know that human beings are complex and perceive risk differently. This means that decisions are often not rational. Some would say that when people talk about risks, they are predictably irrational (Ariely, 2009). That's what makes facilitating risk management such an interesting challenge.

What will you gain from reading this book?

This book is designed to be a helpful companion to you as you manage risk. It covers seven distinct areas.

Groups involved in risk management need to understand what they're working on and what level of detail they need to go to? Chapter 2 provides a broad overview of the field of risk management, including key elements of process and how people fit. Use this to refresh your own understanding and decide what to share with the people you're supporting.

Because people are 'predicably irrational' (Ariely, 2009), it is foolish to assume that application of a risk process will give meaningful, reliable outputs. Bias is inherent and must be acknowledged and dealt with as far as practicable. Chapter 3 provides more detail on this. It can all sound impossible, but there are practical things you can do to address inherent biases.

Whether risk facilitation is just a small part of your job or takes up 100 per cent of your time, Chapter 4 will give you an overview of the skills you need. Stories from successful risk facilitators show how they've delivered results inside their organisations. You'll gain ideas on how best to develop your own skills, as well as possible development paths for your organisation.

Chapter 5 includes each step of the risk management process, showing how you can break it down into simple steps. We provide proven practices for each step, showing how you can use the right mix of workshops, small groups, and individual work to keep people engaged and to get results from start to finish.

Chapter 6 covers the whole area of making risk workshops work. It gives a range of practical tips to help you get the best from your groups.

The days have long gone when meetings and workshops were always conducted with everyone in the same physical room at the same time. Hybrid working, where some people are together in the same space and others are elsewhere, and remote working, where all are dispersed geographically, are both commonplace. Chapter 7 brings together our best advice on making virtual risk management work, whether you are hybrid or fully remote.

In this book, we've identified a whole host of traps for the unwary. These are the pitfalls that we've had to overcome ourselves and we've helped our clients with. By reading this book, especially Chapter 8, you'll know what to avoid and, more importantly, *how*. We trust that you'll be better prepared, able to use your knowledge with individuals and groups, avoiding skewed results.

And overall . . .

Above all this book is a practical, quick read. It's full of tips that you can put into practice straight away, confident that they are based on practical experience, as well as research. In addition to our own experience, you'll see real-life stories from other people who are trying to make risk management work and hear the pitfalls they have encountered.

Why read this book now?

The first edition of this book was written in 2011 as the global economy was recovering from shocks to banking systems. As we complete this second edition, we are over two years into dealing with a global pandemic. Many feel that the credit crunch of the late 2000s and the massive human and economic costs of the pandemic are a direct result of poor, uncontrolled risk management underpinned by sustained false optimism around the world. Whether this is true or not, it is a fact that uncertainty is all around us, and we need to be able to work out which uncertainties matter to our objectives and then take appropriate action.

It is well accepted that a focus on process alone won't make risk management work and that skilled facilitation of risk is needed to make sure good decisions are taken in risky and important situations. This is the case whether you're thinking about your work, your family, your community, or your individual objectives.

Bringing together Ruth's expertise in risk management and Penny's expertise in facilitation, this book gives you a practical guide to make sure you can make risk management work in the places you work and play.

Over to you

This book is designed to help you to tap into the latest understanding of risk management and facilitation and to apply many practical ideas and tips. Please let us know how the ideas and tips work for you. We'd welcome your input and any changes you would suggest for future editions. You can contact us via the website that accompanies this book and download further resources at www.makingriskwork.com.

Questions for reflection

1. To what extent is risk management working for you now?
2. Is risk management different at work, at home or in a community setting?
3. What makes it different?

Reference and further reading

Ariely, D. (2009). *Predictably irrational: The hidden forces that shape our decisions*. HarperCollins.

2 What is risk management?

In this chapter we want to explore what risk management means for practitioners. If risk management is going to work, then there are some things that must be in place – we'll point out what they are.

People and their organisations can often become fixated on formal risk management methods, process, and tools. This is clear from looking at the topics covered in conferences or by reading magazines and books on the subject.

Organisations have spent a small fortune setting up methods, processes, tools, and training; but these things alone do not enable great risk management practice. Risk management is difficult in practice because it relies on getting groups of people to agree on how to manage things in the future, things that only *may* happen. It is often counter-intuitive for people to spend their valuable time *now* considering things that only *might* happen in the future. Getting groups of people to agree how to do this is even more challenging. Different people have different perceptions, preconceptions, and hang-ups about what might happen and what matters most. Facilitation is really important here in order to engage and encourage people with different viewpoints to work together effectively.

DOI: 10.4324/9781003245858-2

The chapter is split into five sections. We will:

1. Give you an overview of the words people use in *describing risk management*, both informally and formally
2. Outline for you the *fundamentals of risk assessment*
3. Show you why *people and their opinions matter*
4. Help you to understand the essential steps in *responding to risks wisely*
5. Provide for you some tips on *keeping risk management alive*.

Describing risk management

Although people have been managing risk forever, there are still good reasons why some sort of process is needed in organisations. First and foremost, though, think about risk management as a natural human process. If you reflect on what you and others do naturally, it can help to find ways of making risk management successful in work and group situations.

People are all great risk managers, or we wouldn't have come so far along life's pathway, largely intact and unscathed.

So why do organisations need to develop a systematic, formal process for risk management? There are two primary reasons.

1. To help make plans and forecasts about the future as robust as possible. Plans include bids for external work, requests for internal funding, and setting expectations about results. Plans outline what will be done, to what standards, when, and for how much.
2. To make a connection between all the personal intuitive assessments of risk that exist to try to establish a common understanding of how to proceed across the organisation.

The need for a consistent, shared, and organised approach in organisations has brought a degree of formality to a natural process. As members of organisations, we have little option but to go with this, but it's good to hold on to the knowledge that each one of us is a naturally capable risk manager.

We can't talk about risk without using words like 'chance' and 'consequence':

- What's the chance that *x* will happen?
- If I take the chance, what might the consequence be?

This simple concept can seem more complicated when words such as 'probability' or 'likelihood' are used instead of 'chance', or when 'impact' or 'effect' are used to mean the same as 'consequence'.

People also talk about 'risk', 'a risk', 'the risk', what is 'at risk', or 'that's risky'. There are many parts of speech all referring to things that might happen that would matter to us if they did.

Processes developed by professional bodies, regulators, and standards organisations have tried to define terms using a common language. You can judge from reviewing Table 2.1 whether this has been successful. The table lists many of the current standards and guides relating to risk management, along with the words they use to describe risk and the risk management process.

In addition to those risk management standards referenced in the table, yet more exist. These include documents that describe the language used, for example, in financial services or subject specialisms such as health and safety, business continuity, or insurance. There is also national and international guidance and legislation that requires companies to manage risk at a corporate level such as the UK Corporate Governance Code, the US legislation known as Sarbanes Oxley or SOx, or the European Basel Accord (currently Basel III). If you want to know more about these then an internet search will help you out.

Table 2.1 Comparison of risk management standards

	Definition of risk	Risk management process	Unique aspects and emphasis
Management of Risk – Guidance for Practitioners (M_o_R), Fourth edition (2022)	An uncertain event or set of events that, should it occur, will have an effect on the achievement of objectives. Risk is a neutral concept; risks can either be threats (downside risks) or opportunities (upside risks).	A Define context and objectives B Identify threats and opportunities C Prioritise risks D Assess combined risk profile E Plan responses F Agree contingency G Monitor and report progress H Review and adapt	• Entire chapters on risk principles and people considerations • Applicable to strategic, portfolio, programme, project, product, and operational risk • Part of a larger suite of guidance including Managing Successful Programmes and PRINCE2
ISO 31000:2018 Risk management – guidelines (2018)	Effect of uncertainty on objectives	A Scope, context, and criteria B Risk identification C Risk analysis D Risk evaluation E Risk treatment F Monitoring and review G Recording and reporting H Communication and consultation	• Applicable to all levels of risk management • Includes risk principles and a risk management framework • Lists communication and consultation as distinct element of the process

(Continued)

10 What is risk management?

Table 2.1 (Continued)

	Definition of risk	Risk management process	Unique aspects and emphasis
PMI Standard for Risk Management in Portfolios, Programs and Projects (2019)	An uncertain event or condition that, if it occurs, has a positive or negative effect on one or more enterprise, portfolio, programme, and project objectives	A Plan risk management B Identify risks C1 Perform qualitative risk analysis C2 Perform quantitative risk analysis D Plan risk responses F Implement risk responses E/G Monitor risks	
Risk Analysis and Management for Projects [RAMP] – Third edition (2014)	A possible occurrence which could affect (positively or negatively) the achievement of the objectives for an investment	A Process launch B Plan and initiate risk review C Identify risks D Evaluate risks E Devise measures for responding to risks F Assess residual risks and decide whether to continue G Plan responses to residual risks H Communicate risk response strategy and response plan I Implement strategy and plans J Control risks K Process close-down	• Considers opportunities as well as threats • Focus is on whole life assets, with emphasis on capital projects

What is risk management? 11

Project Risk Analysis and Management [PRAM] Guide – Second edition (2004)	**Risk event** An uncertain event or set of circumstances that, should it or they occur, would have an effect on the achievement of one or more of the project's objectives **Project risk** The exposure of stakeholders to the consequences of variations in outcome	A Initiate B Identify C Assess D Plan responses E Implement responses F Manage process	• Includes chapters on the role of the risk management benefits, links to governance and assurance, risk manager, risk facilitation, reference class forecasting, risk management in iterative life cycles, and risk management is specific industry sectors • Defines risk at two levels: risk event and project risk
BS IEC 62198:2014 – Managing risk in projects – Application guidelines (2014)	Combination of the probability of an event occurring and its consequences on project objectives	A Establishing the context B Risk identification C Risk analysis D Risk evaluation E Risk treatment F Monitoring and review G Post project	• Originated as part of dependability standard • Focus on projects with technological content

Source: updated by Murray-Webster from an original in Hillson & Simon, 2020

Fundamentals of risk assessment

What is risk?

One of the first things to think about is the difference between uncertainty and risk. Uncertainty and risk are different. Many things are uncertain, not all of them are risks. Uncertainties only become risks when they could affect our objectives. "Risks are uncertainties that matter" (Hillson & Murray-Webster, 2007).

It is also really important not to become confused between risks and issues. Issues are problems that are happening now. There is nothing uncertain about them at all. Risks may become issues. Issues may be causes of risks, so there is a link between them – but it's critical that they're not managed in the same way.

Risk – good, bad, or both?

Contrary to English dictionary definitions, risks are not necessarily negative – threats to our objectives. Some of the situations that are uncertain would result in a beneficial outcome should they occur.

For example, the currency exchange rate when I go on holiday may be more favourable to me than the rate I used when budgeting. To get the best out of risk management it's important to focus not just on potential *problems, but also potential opportunities* – downsides and upsides.

How much risk can you tolerate?

It's also really important to know how much risk you are comfortable with. This applies to you as an individual as well as to your project or department. Practitioners who talk about this concept use three slightly different, but linked terms – risk capacity, risk appetite, and risk tolerance.

So you'll need to answer questions such as "How much risk do we have the capacity and resources to bear?" and "How 'hungry' are we for risk within that capacity?" "Are we able to make some risky choices because the potential prize is greater than the potential loss?" or "Have we taken on enough risk already and don't have an appetite or a capacity for more?" Answering these questions will allow you to define the tolerances that we are prepared to accept for a particular activity.

> A simple home example might be related to a family holiday in the sun. Most of us are not likely to have the *capacity* and resources to book alternative flights if we miss the one we are booked on. On that understanding, we are not likely to have much of an *appetite* for taking risks that would cause us to miss our flight, so we set *tolerances* around the time we leave for the airport that provide us some contingency. We may spend too long in airports (and some would say that provides the opportunity for shopping), but we don't take too many chances related to the primary objective.

A critical first step in risk management is to define the organisation's *risk capacity, risk appetite,* and therefore the *risk tolerances* for the work they're doing. This is an activity that must be done by the senior management of the organisational unit in question. That could be the executive management team for a whole organisation or it might be a departmental team, programme sponsoring group, or similar. Helping senior teams through this first decision-making process is a task where experienced risk facilitators can help enormously.

What's risky and why?

Too often organisations have lists of risks where the associated descriptions tell us very little about the situation. If you can understand the cause of a risk, you may be able to avoid it entirely (for a threat) or exploit it (for an opportunity).

It is vitally important to describe risks well if we are to make good assessments of their relative priority. Think about describing risks in a way that distinguishes between the cause (a fact), the risk event (which isn't a fact), and the impact on objectives (why it matters).

An example of a positive risk (potential opportunity) might be:

> Cause: Because business is slower this year than last year and staff have more time
> Risk: The company may be able to generate greater brand awareness by exploiting new e-marketing skills
> Impact on objectives: Resulting in increased sales.

An example of a negative risk (threat) might be:

> Cause: Because business is slower this year than last year and staff have more time

Risk: Staff may become demotivated and less effective
Impact on objectives: Resulting in an accelerated decline in sales.

Can you see the cause, the risk event, and the effect in each of these? Being able to turn vague expressions of risk into specific risk descriptions, as shown in the examples, is a fundamental step toward effective risk assessment.

Another good reason for describing risks well is to encourage people to think about *why* their situation is risky in the first place.

With some risks we can calculate the odds with certainty – situations like playing the lottery and other games of pure chance. Risks in business are fundamentally different. When playing the lottery, it's possible to calculate the exact chance of winning. In business, there is no situation that is a game of pure chance because there are always other factors that we don't know enough about; yet they are influential. When situations are ambiguous it is impossible to calculate probabilities with precision – we can only make our most educated guess. This means that judgements about risk are highly subjective.

How much does each risk matter?

Even though judgements about the chance of a particular risk occurring are subjective, we still need to make these judgements so we can prioritise risks and decide which ones warrant management rather than leaving the situation to chance. Prioritisation is typically done by combining the assessment of probability (the chance that the uncertainty will become fact) with a judgement of how much the risk would impact our objectives. Here we are guessing, too. However, we can make these guesses more 'educated' by defining specific criteria for what makes a risk on a particular objective high, medium, or low.

16   What is risk management?

Because human assessments of probability and impact are educated guesses, it's important to avoid relying on any one individual's opinion. Where there's relevant data that can be used it should be – but often data about the past isn't that relevant in predicting the future. For example, just because the last three summers have been wet it doesn't help us predict the weather this summer. We need to prioritise risks as objectively as possible – on the basis of their likelihood and the scale of their impact. Some organisations present the prioritisation of individual risks visually on a grid – often called a probability/impact grid, a risk assessment matrix, a heat map, or other similar title. Other organisations use a simple calculation of expected monetary value (EMV) to cost each risk, allowing a financial prioritisation. This is done by estimating the most likely cost of the impact should the risk event occur, then calculating a percentage of this impact cost based on the estimated probability. This is not a precise science but allows risks to be compared using a monetary value.

How risky is this situation?

When each of the identified risks has been assessed for probability and impact, you have a prioritisation based on the chance of each risk event happening and the consequences if it did. This list is usually structured as a risk log or risk register, or in larger organisations in a risk database.

Such a prioritisation is useful, of course, but you can't judge the overall riskiness of the situation from a simple list of discrete risks. To assess riskiness relies on using techniques that allow you to look at the combined effect of individual risks on the overall objectives. The outputs from this analysis show how much the objectives are exposed to risk, and they are useful for a number of purposes. These include:

- Making provision for a contingency budget (risk reserve)
- Shaping bids – either for internal funding or to win client work
- Discussing confidence levels in estimates with stakeholders.

Some organisations use sophisticated modelling and simulation techniques to support their risk-based decision-making. Describing the mathematics underpinning such techniques is out of scope of this book on facilitation; however, the techniques rely on the availability of good input data to help people make appropriate decisions. Unfortunately, Penny and Ruth see far too many situations where 'garbage in' gives 'garbage out' no matter how sophisticated the process in between. What's even more dangerous is when people believe that the 'garbage out' is good information! The risk facilitator can play a vital role in organisations that use risk-modelling techniques. They can help the decision-making team to challenge the assumptions underpinning the data and to carry out analyses that provide good information on which to base risky and important business decisions.

People and their opinions matter

Although risk management is a natural skill for most people – there is a complicating factor. Risk is about perception. Ruth's perception of what is risky is different from Penny's perception. Put ten people in a room and present them with the same information, and you will get ten different views of what the risks are, how likely they are to occur, and how much they'd matter if they did. We all have a different risk attitude. So although the risk management process is largely common sense, it is not easy to get shared views. Adding more people increases the range of views!

18 *What is risk management?*

Ruth's work with David Hillson on understanding and managing risk attitude (Murray-Webster & Hillson, 2008, 2021; Hillson & Murray-Webster, 2007) explains the large number of factors that have the power to influence perceptions. Chapter 3 focuses on some of these. These perceptions affect assessments of risk because they determine the choices that different people adopt in risky situations. One example is the impact of positive experience on the perception of risks. If I've enjoyed doing something risky in the past, I'm likely to downplay the risks in a future, similar situation and believe that I can manage anything adverse that may occur. The reverse also applies. If we have no experience, or have had a bad experience in the past, most people are likely to be more cautious in future. This is one of a huge number of influences on human perception of risk and riskiness. More will be explored later in the book but for now it can be useful to think about the influences on perception of risk as falling into three groups as shown below.

Have I seen this before?

What is my automatic reaction?

How do I feel about it?

How I perceive the risk

The three groups of influences (called the 'triple strand' in Murray-Webster and Hillson's work) combine so that at the point where each of us makes a judgement about a risk, the strands are tightly intertwined, making it quite difficult to distinguish the particular influences that have led to our opinion. In situations that are particularly risky and important, people, or teams of people, need to have the skills to unpick the triple strand and check that the chosen response to the risk is appropriate in the situation. Some people have the personal skills to test their assumptions in this way or to help their team do this. Many don't and benefit greatly from support from a skilled facilitator who demonstrates the qualities shown below. We have found that great facilitators can 'read' a situation well, and through a combination of seeing, hearing, and feeling, can work out how to balance the needs of the situation.

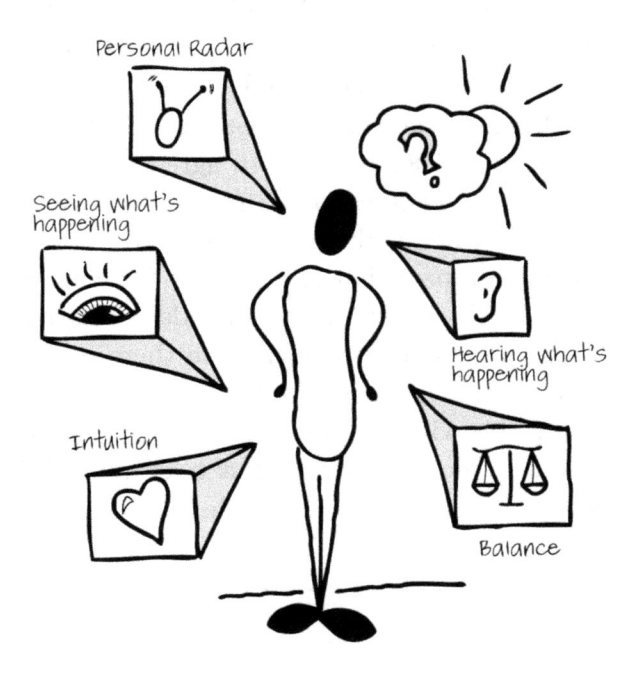

Risk attitude labels

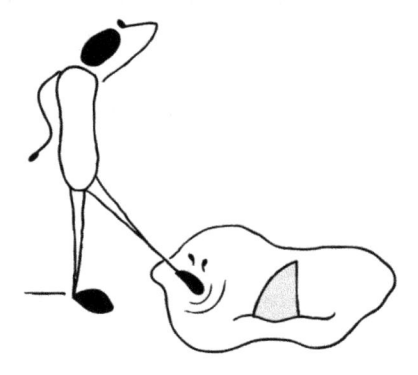

20 What is risk management?

It is common for people to use labels such as risk averse, risk tolerant, or risk seeking to describe the risk attitude of individuals, groups, organisations, and even nations. What do these labels mean in practice?

We adopt the definition of risk attitude from Ruth's books with David Hillson, that is, "chosen response to a risk, driven by perception". Risk attitudes, held by individuals or groups, are situational. We each have different chosen responses to different risks at different times. Penny and Ruth can both agree that they are much more risk averse when it comes to taking risks with their children's safety than they are when making business choices. But what does risk averse mean? Simply it is the degree of the comfort with the perceived level of risk. A risk-averse attitude is relatively uncomfortable with the perceived level of risk so there is motivation to try to make the situation more certain. A risk-seeking attitude is relatively comfortable with the perceived level of risk so there is no motivation to create more certainty. Risk tolerant and risk-neutral attitudes are also described below in Table 2.2.

Table 2.2 Risk attitude labels

Term	Definition
Risk averse	Uncomfortable with uncertainty, desire to avoid or reduce threats and exploit opportunities to remove uncertainty. Would be unhappy with an uncertain outcome.
Risk seeking	Comfortable with uncertainty, no desire to avoid or reduce threats or to exploit opportunities to remove uncertainty. Would be happy with an uncertain outcome.
Risk tolerant	Tolerant of uncertainty, no strong desire to respond to threats or opportunities in any way. Could tolerate an uncertain outcome if necessary.
Risk neutral	Uncomfortable with uncertainty in the long term so prepared to take whatever short-term actions are necessary to deliver a certain long-term outcome.

Source: Murray-Webster & Hillson, 2008

Responding to risks wisely

Identifying risks associated with those objectives that matter most to us, describing them well, and prioritising them are all important parts of the process. When you've done this, you can put together plans and bids for work or funding that address risk explicitly. Some organisations stop here and leave the risks to chance, knowing what they are but not doing anything to try to manage them or increase their beneficial impact on objectives. That's risk assessment with no risk management.

There are other options, typically described as risk response strategies in the books and guides, but colloquially often called 'risk mitigation' by practitioners.

Not just about mitigation!

At this point it's worth stating that, in Ruth and Penny's opinion, using the term mitigation in all cases is not that helpful. Mitigation, derived from the old English verb to 'soften' and defined in dictionaries as "to reduce, makes less severe, or render less harsh or hostile" is *one* approach to dealing with a downside risk or threat. But there are others as described below – and of course lots of things you can do to make positive risks *more* likely and *more* beneficial should they occur.

So, what are the essential steps when deciding whether or not to act to respond to a particular risk?

Ownership

The first thing that must be done is to make sure that the risk has an owner – a named person who is best placed to make decisions about how to manage the risk. When talking to practitioners during the writing of this book, Ruth and Penny have heard many concerns about the lack of clear ownership for specific risks. This is of concern. If a risk is real and worthy of assessment and management then a person who cares (or is paid to care) about the impact the risk could have on objectives must take ownership of that risk. The risk owner is then the person who makes the decisions about *if and how* to respond to the risk.

These are the options open to you as a risk owner:

- Take the risk
- Prepare a plan B
- Treat the risk
- Share (not transfer)
- Make it certain.

Each option is described here.

Take the risk

You could accept the risk. Accepting a risk doesn't mean doing nothing, as every risk needs to be monitored to make sure it doesn't creep up and surprise you, but it does mean not spending any time and money now to try to make the situation more certain. Often called the 'accept' strategy – it's all about being willing to let the uncertainty play out.

Prepare a plan B

Accepting the risk without any preparation for what you'd do if the risk did occur can be simply irresponsible, especially if the risk will have a highly positive or highly negative impact on your objectives. One response strategy that is not often described, but we believe is a very natural approach, is to *accept the risk – for now* – but spend a little time and effort putting in place a 'plan B'. A plan B is a simple way of referring to what you will do *if* the risk materialises, for example, having spare clothes in your hand-luggage in case your checked luggage doesn't arrive with you in time for an important meeting. Some of the standards and guides talk about plan Bs as contingent plans, fallback plans, or real options. Real options are interesting since they buy you flexibility to decide whether to spend money now or at a later date – but with the knowledge that the plan B is in place. We think this response option is an instinctive one used often in our lives but is not considered enough in work situations.

Both the 'take' or 'accept' strategy and the 'prepare' strategy as described above don't tend to require large investments of time and money now. Other strategies are likely to require bigger immediate investments, and so they need to be thought through carefully and costed so that the organisation knows that the response delivers value for money. Some people find it very counter-intuitive to spend time and money now on a situation that may not happen anyway; however, the whole business case for risk management is that overall it's cheaper to prevent than cure.

Treat the risk

For some significant risks, the best option may be to try to reduce the uncertainty in some way. Treating a negative threat is where the word mitigate applies! You are trying to *reduce* probability, *reduce* impact, or both. Treating a positive, potential opportunity is usually referred to as the 'enhance' strategy and involves trying to increase probability, impact, or both.

Share (not transfer)

One way of treating a risk is to share the risk with others. This can be done in the supply chain, sharing a risk with a customer or supplier, so the impact of any loss/pain or gain is not with one party. For example, if bad weather prevents progress on the building of a new extension at home, the costs of paying the staff could be shared between you and your builder. We like the word 'share' as an alternative to the word 'transfer' that is often used. Although insurance can be seen as a form of risk transfer, we argue you can never transfer all the risk to another party. Someone else might pay the costs if the risk occurs, but inevitably there'll be some impact on your objectives too, for example extra time. This point is all too clear in Ruth's mind having spent a whole weekend sorting out her cellar following a flood. The insurance paid for damage, but not Ruth's time in sorting out all the messy bits!

Sharing risk is a good thing to do and lots of contracts are now set up on a pain share/gain share basis to do just that. *It is important to beware of the 'transfer' word* – particularly when working with suppliers and customers in the supply chain. As noted by official bodies such as the UK Government (2020), attempting to transfer risk in the supply chain tends to destroy trust and can result in people padding their estimates more and more. Smart organisations are starting to realise that. Although risk transfer is a potential option in some situations, it should only be done with eyes open to the potential consequences of doing so.

As highlighted in all of response strategies mentioned so far, a *residual risk* remains if the response strategy has been to take the risk, prepare a plan B, treat the risk, share the risk, or transfer the risk. Most of these generic responses will have changed either the assessment of probability, the assessment of impact, or both. There will still be a residual risk that means that there is still some probability of the threat or opportunity having an impact on objectives.

Make it certain

You could argue the first thing to consider is whether or not you can do something to eliminate the risk altogether – so there is no residual risk. This is one of the reasons why describing risks in a three-part way – the cause, the risk event, and the effect – is so powerful. If you can get rid of the cause of a threat, the risk has gone. If you can make the cause of an opportunity completely certain, you've got it. Making a potential problem or a potential opportunity certain is often called the 'terminate option'. You may find it more helpful to talk about *avoiding* threats and *exploiting* opportunities. Sometimes it might cost lots of time and money to do this, yet it's still worth it. Sometimes just thinking about the situation in a different way can have the same result for no additional cost.

And be careful!

The trick with all these response strategies is to avoid planning actions that would make the situation even more risky. The technical term for this is 'secondary risk'. In common parlance we'd talk about not 'jumping from the frying pan into the fire' or 'throwing the baby out with the bath water'. An example might be reducing the risk of your children becoming injured in the park by not letting them play outside with their friends at all. In avoiding one risk (your children being injured, or worse), you introduce bigger risks associated with health, socialisation, and general 'street-wise' skills. So, when you've planned risk responses, make sure you add any secondary threats or opportunities to the risk register and assess the chance and impact of them occurring in the usual way. This way you can make sure that risk responses don't have unintended consequences.

Keeping risk management alive

Any risk assessment and management plan is only a snapshot in time. As the work progresses, new information might come to light, situations change, or new people join the team. The situation is dynamic not static, so risk management needs to keep pace.

The best type of risk management is where the whole team, top to bottom, lives the process. Where this happens, discussions about potential opportunities and potential problems are part of day-to-day conversations as well as being embedded in the formal governance and decision-making processes. The risk register is 'alive', and the team embrace the process because they know it adds considerable value.

The worst type of risk management is the 'tick-box' compliance type, where risk registers are only completed or updated just before an audit or when the customer asks to see it. This sort of behaviour devalues what can be a massively useful process. We've observed that when 'lip service' is paid to the risk management process the result is a sapping of energy and a creation of a cynicism that is difficult for organisations to break.

One point of view is that a compliance mentality to risk management is of no value – possibly worse than doing nothing at all and leaving the risk to chance. Why? Because leaving it all to chance does not incur the costs of 'pretending' to do risk management. For the costs of applying risk management to deliver a return on investment, a supportive culture is required.

In the final analysis, many individuals manage risk intuitively – they always have and will. However, in situations where there is a 'tick-box' approach, the organisation is unlikely to get any of the formal benefits and so may as well spend its time doing something else.

For organisations that can overcome a compliance mentality and do risk management well, the benefits from risk management are threefold:

1 *Less waste* (problems that could have been foreseen, missed opportunities, rework, and hassle)
2 *More confidence* (in plans, forecasts, and relationships because there are fewer surprises)
3 *Better decisions* (because decision-making is based on the best possible information – not just about what is but about what might be).

In order to move from a situation where risk assessments are done once, or infrequently, to a situation where risk management is at the forefront of the minds of managers and staff, our advice is to keep a *focus on the benefits*. The three areas of benefit listed above have an impact on individuals as well as the organisation as a whole. Developing measures that allow a continual focus on the benefits of risk management really help build a culture where risk management is alive – with 'evergreen' risk registers and proactive behaviours.

Developing suitable performance-based measures that show how risk management helps is sometimes a challenge for organisations. One of the challenges to overcome is the fact that a problem avoided isn't very visible. There's nothing tangible to measure when something doesn't happen. However, trends can be measured, for example, waste can be *tracked over time*. With improved risk management there should be a downward trend in the cost of waste. Remember the simple calculation of expected monetary value (EMV) for each risk, explained earlier in this chapter. Many organisations use this to track how well the overall riskiness of the work is reduced over time. Another way is to track time spent on rework, or other wasteful actions that could have been foreseen and prevented by proactive risk management.

Confidence and the strength of relationships can also be tracked through customer and staff surveys or 'voice of the client' focus groups. Clients who lack confidence will tend to micromanage or be overly contractual about issues. The same is true for internal managers. I'm sure we can all think of how our behaviour is affected when there is confidence in a relationship, as opposed to no confidence. It is to be expected that behaviour will be influenced by surprises, irrespective of whether they are nasty ones that hurt (actually or metaphorically) or the knowledge of a missed opportunity. What effective risk management can enable is confidence that surprises will be minimised and therefore relationships flourish and grow within teams across businesses and supply chains. This is because people will be working well together to anticipate potential problems and opportunities. Their confidence and success will grow as the number of issues and problems diminish.

Whatever indicators or measures you use to keep the focus on the benefits of risk management, the key from our point of view is that at least some of these are measuring trends. Trends give you information on the degree to which risk management is dynamic, alive, well, and adding tangible value over time. Taking the time to gather this data really helps to move risk management away from the 'tickbox' compliance arena that so many practitioners complain about.

Summary

In this chapter, we've explained how risk management comes naturally to people and is a key part of general life as well as business. We've also outlined the steps in the risk process and the key things to be aware of. Although, at one level, good risk management seems to be common sense, experience says that it isn't common practice. We've covered a whole range of complicating factors that explain why this is so. You'll need to be aware of these to be a great facilitator of risk and get the best out of the people you are supporting.

So, what does it take to be a great facilitator of risk? Chapter 4 describes the role of the facilitator in general; Chapter 5 will show the many ways in which facilitators can support the risk process described in this chapter in different organisational settings and contexts. Many people associate risk facilitation with risk workshops. We argue that the risk workshop is only one part of risk facilitation, albeit an important one. Workshops are the subject of Chapter 6, with virtual working, whether fully remote or hybrid, the subject of Chapter 7. Chapter 8 then lists the challenges that practitioners have told us they experience. We respond to each of these pitfalls before closing this book with our ten golden guidelines for risk facilitators in Chapter 9. Next, however, we take a deeper look at people, their perceptions, and why they matter so much to effective risk management.

Questions for reflection

1. Which parts of risk management do you understand and have confidence working with and which parts are troublesome?
2. How does the (possibly) more formal language in your workplace relate to the language used in the chapter?
3. What have you noticed about how this description of risk differs from what you are used to?
4. What are your thoughts about the human aspects of risk management?

References and further reading

Hillson, D. A., & Murray-Webster, R. (2007). *Understanding and managing risk attitude* (2nd ed.). Gower.

Hillson, D. A., & Simon, P. W. (2020). *Practical project risk management: The ATOM methodology* (3rd ed.). Management Concepts.

HM Government. (2020). *The sourcing and consultancy playbooks*. Retrieved January 18, 2022, from www.gov.uk/government/publications/the-sourcing-and-consultancy-playbooks

Murray-Webster, R., & Hillson, D. A. (2008). *Managing group risk attitude*. Gower.

Murray-Webster, R., & Hillson, D. A. (2021). *Making risky and important decisions: A leader's guide*. CRC Press.

3 Why people and their perceptions matter

In Chapter 2, we started to explore why people and their perceptions matter. This chapter will help you to understand more, so you can figure out the best way to deal with the individuals and groups you work with.

Start by thinking about decisions. People make them all the time; in fact, it's suggested by some that people make up to 2000 decisions per hour – that's a decision every 2 seconds! To be able to do that we have adapted to make most of these decisions subconsciously and habitually. For example, we do not have to give conscious thought to decide how to brush our teeth in the morning. Not all of these habitual decisions are risky and important – but some are – like driving a car, crossing the road, spending scarce resources like money and time, and speaking to the people we care most about. In a business context, decisions matter to a varying degree too. No decision is risk-free, many of them are important and all are made by people.

It's also probably worth considering that when we make a decision we have no idea how things will turn out. Sometimes, we make a poor decision and ignore the risks, but we're lucky and everything turns out okay. Sometimes, we make a good decision and take a balanced view of the risks, but we're unlucky – other things happen out of our control, and we don't meet our objective.

32 *Why people and their perceptions matter*

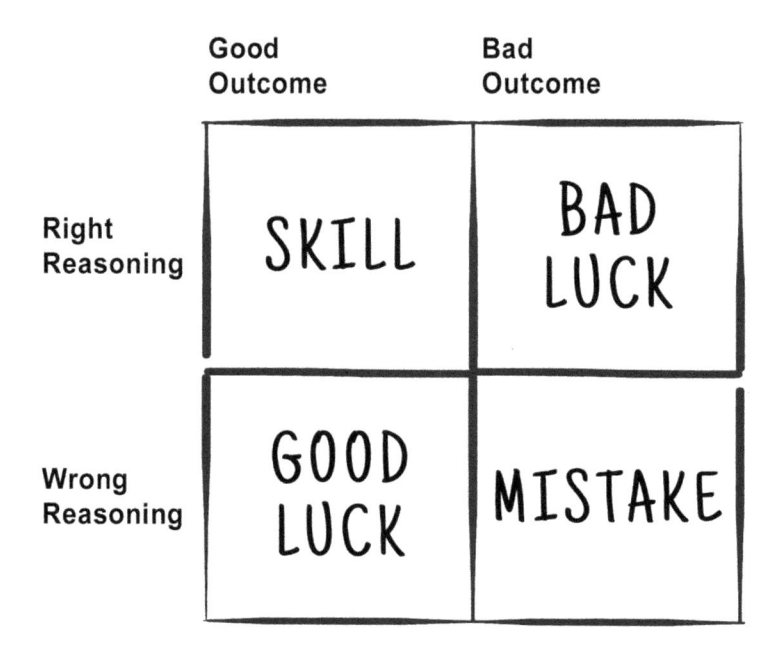

	Good Outcome	Bad Outcome
Right Reasoning	SKILL	BAD LUCK
Wrong Reasoning	GOOD LUCK	MISTAKE

Figure 3.1 Good decisions are based on right reasoning

In a world that is risky, and indeed some would say volatile, uncertain, complex, and ambiguous (VUCA), there are no risk-free decisions and no certain outcomes. We tread a path balancing risk and reward (the achievement of our objectives). As facilitators of risk, we help the people we live and work with do the same.

CONSCIOUS
Have I seen this before?

SUBCONSCIOUS
What is my automatic reaction?

AFFECTIVE
How do I feel about it?

How I perceive the risk

Figure 3.2 The triple strand of influences on perception

We introduced the idea of the triple strand of influences on perception, and therefore the choice of risk attitude in Chapter 2. Let's unpick that a little more.

When we make a decision, as an individual or group, we do that choosing a risk attitude. We may not be aware we have made a choice because we fall back on habits or innate preferences, but nevertheless it is a choice. For any decision, our risk attitude lies on a range between wanting certainty (risk averse) or 'rolling with' the uncertainty (risk seeking).

The risk attitudes we choose are influenced (you could say biased) by many things. In the triple strand idea, we categorise these into three influences:

- Conscious: have I seen anything like this before
- Subconscious: what is my automatic reaction
- Affective: how to I feel about this situation?

In the remainder of this chapter, we'll explore the things that bias our judgement and why, and we'll address what we can do to minimise bias when it really matters.

How are we biased?

Conscious factors: have I seen anything like this before?

Conscious factors are those things that can be seen, counted, measured, and/or observed in a physical sense. They are not always facts, but the chance of them occurring can be worked out in a rational way, and their impact on our objectives can be estimated.

> **Proximity**, the closeness in time and space, is a conscious factor that can influence us in a number of ways. We tend to give

preference to things that are close. We find it easier to deprioritise things that are far away. The proverb 'out of sight, out of mind' warns us of the risks of being biased by proximity.
- **Manageability** is another factor at the conscious level. In one sense, it is very logical to prioritise activities where we feel confident that we know what to do. Our pre-existing skills, knowledge, and experience help us judge whether a situation happening now will be manageable or not. We can do the same for a potential situation in the future where risk might occur. We are biased to prefer the things we judge will be manageable, even though this might be at the expense of better options.

Other conscious, situational factors include:

- The **urgency** of a decision or activity, where we are typically biased to assume that things are important, just because they are urgent – this may not be the case
- The potential **benefits** of a project, where we are typically biased to believe that advantageous scenarios are likely to occur
- The potential **range of impacts** of a risk, where we tend to be biased to discount potential outcomes at the extremes of a range, i.e. ignoring the tail of a distribution.

Perceptions influenced by conscious factors are the easiest to challenge and change because they are conscious – we talk about them and sometimes we measure them, as they are accessible. Unfortunately, though, we are also influenced by factors that are hidden: subconscious factors.

Subconscious factors: What is my automatic reaction?

We will start with technical language because you may hear these words in various situations.

Heuristics

Heuristics provide one way to bias us subconsciously. Heuristics are often described as 'mental short-cuts' or 'rules of thumb'. The human brain has developed them to be efficient and to thrive, sometimes even to survive. For example, the **availability heuristic** is the brain's way of making most recent data most memorable to us. If we're in a situation that we have encountered many times over many years and that usually was good, but the most recent time was really bad, our automatic assessment of the risk of something bad happening will be high. Colleagues who have had different experiences will have different perceptions. How likely is the risk of something bad happening again this time? How bad might it be? There is no right answer, and worse, different people will have different views based on past experience.

There are many known heuristics that have been identified by people who study the brain and behaviour. Each works in a slightly different way, but each has the potential to skew our perceptions and therefore choices in risky and important situations.

Below are some of the common heuristics and how they work to bias our thinking. You'll notice that some heuristics influence groups of people as well as the individuals in the group.

STEREOTYPING (OFFICIALLY KNOWN AS THE REPRESENTATIVENESS HEURISTIC)

How it works: our brain notices that it's seen something like this before, so assumes as a shortcut that this time it's the same as last time. An example might be a judgement that: 'It's always difficult working with this supplier' when the person who caused problems in the past has left the business. This can lead to terrible errors of judgement about people and their character and likely behaviours that we have prejudged in a stereotypical way. The heuristic applies to situations as well as people. It leads to prejudice.

CONFIRMATION TRAP

How it works: our brain selectively looks for evidence to support earlier judgements and then when the only evidence we perceive confirms our earlier position it reinforces it – we are right – it's true. An example might be a student's decision to start smoking, despite knowing that it is harmful to health, but all around they see other students doing the same, so it must be okay. Such selective perception can lead to 'self-fulfilling prophecies' where a person says something will happen, and then it does happen because only information that supported the prediction was taken into account. It leads, at its worst, to 'I told you so'!

ANCHORING

How it works: our brain remembers and 'anchors to' available data and attaches sometimes illogical significance to that data. You could think of it as 'first impressions last'. The best examples are how sales techniques such as advertising recommended retail prices are designed to anchor and reinforce the anchor so that even if we move, it's only a small adjustment away from the first impression. It leads, at its worst, to very poor decisions being made about how much things will cost, how long things will take to complete, or the quality of a product or service.

GROUPTHINK

How it works: people are social beings who typically value social cohesion in decision-making situations more than getting the right answer. Groupthink works to lead the group to believe that 'we all think this way – we all agree', even when subsequent research has shown every single member of the group disagreed but didn't want to say so. This leads to bias that could be described as 'safety in numbers'. Other heuristics have been shown to be based on this, for example, a risky shift is where a group takes more and more risky decisions because the group mutually reinforces that this is the right thing to do, even though no individual would do that themselves. A cautious shift is opposite; the group becomes increasingly risk averse because they tell themselves that it is right despite individual views. Groupthink (and risky and cautious shifts) lead, at worst, to decisions being made where everyone says 'we agreed', but no individual takes personal accountability for the decision.

Heuristics – good or bad?

Heuristics are generally good. They allow us to function at a high level, make quick decisions, and be efficient. Heuristics are bad when we blindly follow them when doing a risk assessment. A key part of the facilitation of risk is to help people suspend automatic judgement for long enough to consider whether the heuristic is helping in the situation.

Cognitive bias

Another way we are biased subconsciously is through cognitive biases. A quick search of the internet will reveal a very large number of cognitive biases that have been identified by psychologists, behavioural economists, and others who observe and describe human decision-making.

Where heuristics are often really helpful, cognitive biases are always bad because they systemically lead us to believe things that are possible but not the most probable in a situation. They can make us believe, often with great conviction, things that are not accurate or not the most relevant in a situation.

What is known as the **precautionary principle** is a common cognitive bias that you may recognise. The precautionary principle leads us to pay attention to, and believe, data about bad things that are possible but highly improbable. The precautionary principle can make us frightened, frozen, and unable to act in the best interests of the team (and sometimes ourselves) unless we have a way of bringing the subconscious effects to the conscious level and asking 'is this serving our overall objectives in the right way?'

Another example is the **intelligence trap**. This leads us to believe that if someone can eloquently talk about or debate a situation, they must be right. You will notice this as a systemic bias across our society. Those who can confidently describe a situation, present data, or tell a story in a compelling way are typically believed much more than those who may have more relevant information but struggle to describe it or be able to 'hold the argument'. We train our children to be confident and to 'fake it until you make it'. Sometimes it's the ones who can't describe the situation well, or who are less skilled in arguing their point, who have the most relevant insights.

Below are some of the common cognitive biases and how they work to skew our thinking.

SUNK COST FALLACY

How it works: our brain cannot help but take into account past investments when considering future investments. We think that because we have spent lots of money, say mending an old car, that when the car breaks down again it is still the right decision to spend more because, somehow, we think that not doing so will have wasted the previous investment (but this is 'sunk' – we logically should ignore it). The sunk cost fallacy is very prevalent in all parts of life. It is the bias that underpins the saying 'throwing good money after bad'.

OPTIMISM BIAS

How it works: our brain leads us to believe that we are less likely to experience negative things than we are positive things. So, although we can describe good outcomes and bad outcomes in a situation, we automatically downplay the likelihood of the bad thing happening to us. Optimism bias has become a very well understood cognitive bias in the world of project management because it significantly skews estimates of how long things will take and how much they will cost.

ILLUSION OF CONTROL

How it works: our brain leads us to believe that we can control events more than we actually can. It works by exaggerating our personal influence on a situation and downplaying luck. One of the most obvious examples is when we are driving a car. We have a lucky escape from a situation but put it down to our driving skill. The same happens in lots of situations, and it leads to us then projecting an ability to control future situations that is irrational – often deluded.

LOSS AVERSION

How it works: our brain attributes more value to avoiding making a loss than achieving an equivalent gain. The Nobel Prize winning work of Daniel Kahneman and the late Amos Tversky demonstrated this effect that, when described, is really illogical – yet it can affect us all if we are not aware. Loss aversion would lead us to think that a solution that would save the lives of 40 people in a population of 100 was better than an alternative solution that would lead to 50 out of 100 people dying. The alternative is clearly better – 50 live, 50 die. But framing the first solution as saving 40 lives (rather than 60 dying) is a seriously biasing effect. More on the effects of framing later – this is part of the solution for the facilitator of risk.

Cognitive bias – good or bad?

Cognitive biases always have a negative effect if we are not able to interrupt our automatic response. A key part of the facilitation of risk is to help people become aware of bias and find ways of considering the situation from another angle.

Beyond heuristics and cognitive biases, personality also plays a part. It may be that some people are predisposed, through their personality-based preferences, to be uncomfortable with uncertainty and risk. Others will happily be drawn to embrace risk. Neither of these automatic responses are right every time.

Perceptions influenced by subconscious factors are the most difficult to challenge and change, but it's not impossible. With the right intent, we can hold up the mirror and get a glimpse of where we may be deluding ourselves. Skilled facilitation makes this much easier. More on how we do this later, but first we need to look at the third strand – affective factors or feelings.

Affective factors: How do I feel about the situation?

Not everyone is comfortable talking about feelings. For some people it feels private. For others it feels weak. For others it just feels plain awkward. And then there are those who 'wear their heart on their sleeve' and have a strong feelings preference. Whether you are comfortable or uncomfortable with feelings, it is a fact that strong emotions are arguably the most biasing effect on our perceptions and choices under uncertainty.

To understand why strong emotions have such a biasing effect, we need to dip briefly into the workings of the human brain. While we might like to think of ourselves as completely rational beings, in reality much of our brain runs instinctively – for example, our primal fight, flight, and freeze responses to perceptions of danger.

Our brain also associates emotions with memories, triggering strong associations that inform future perceptions and behaviours. For example, a strong negative memory of being harmed as a child may give us an irrational fear of some situations, or a strong positive memory of being in a particular situation may lead us to believe it's right to repeat the behaviour. This is an open loop system and is continually reinforcing, not always in a rational way.

The frontal lobe of our brain, especially the prefrontal cortex, supervises our rational thinking, but often our instincts and/or emotions are more powerful and usually much faster acting. LeDoux's work on pathways in the brain in response to emotional stimuli shows that the fastest pathway bypasses the cortex (rational thinking) entirely. It takes time for our thinking to catch up (LeDoux, 1996, p. 196).

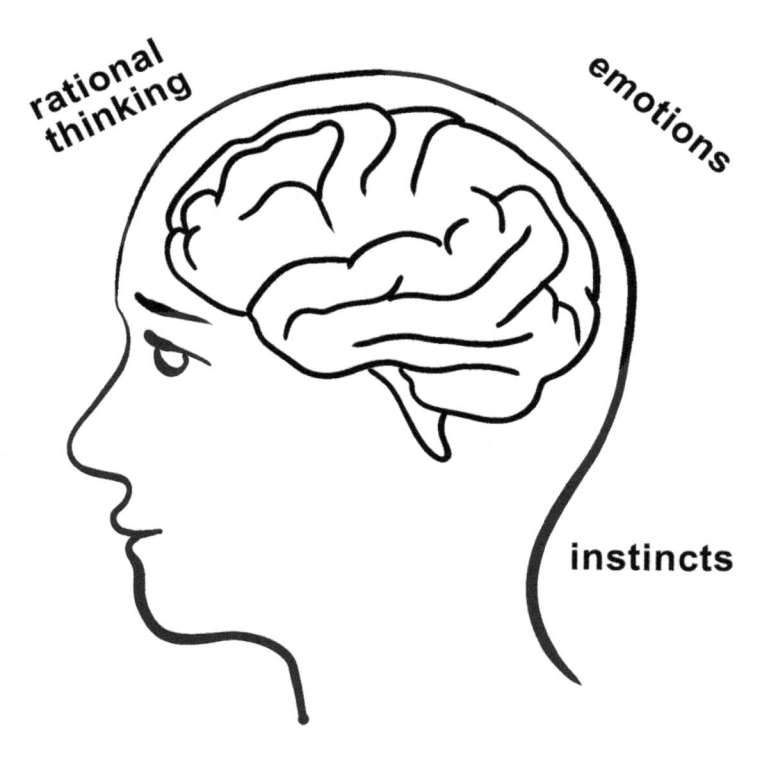

However much we might aspire to be rational thinking machines when it comes to making decisions, the truth is that we are primarily motivated to seek pleasure and avoid pain (Freud & Strachey, 1989). Our brains present us with all sorts of instinctive and emotional triggers that we need to deal with in order to think rationally. Some refer to this as the affect heuristic, the mental shortcut that leads us to rely on our emotions rather than data. This is why some people argue that our emotional quotient, our EQ, is far more impactful in daily life than our intelligence quotient, our IQ.

Fear (and associated emotions such as dread and shame) can be literally or metaphorically paralysing, leading us away from what we want and eroding our ability to achieve our goals. Yet it is rational in the moment because avoiding a situation we fear or are dreading brings us short-term relief, so conforming with the pleasure principle by avoiding pain. Fear leads us to perceive lots of threats and believe them to be really likely to happen and have a bad effect on our objectives.

Love (and associated emotions such as desire and lust) are the opposite effect of fear and dread and lead us toward what we want, irrespective of whether that is wise or not. It is rational in the moment because we are seeking pleasure, but are we aware of the consequences? Love leads us to perceive lots of opportunities and believe them to be really likely to happen and have a great effect on our objectives.

Human emotions are far more subtle than fear/dread/shame or love/desire/lust. But underlying the subtlety of emotions is an underlying motivation to move toward or away from something. This can be counterproductive to good decision-making under uncertainty if not recognised and harnessed.

Back to the triple strand

So, back to the triple strand. At the point of judging a situation and making a decision, an individual will be influenced by a variety of conscious, subconscious, and affective factors. These are largely hidden unless we make a particular effort to stop, reflect, and try to understand. In groups, this is happening to every individual in the group, and there are some particular group effects that also come into play, like groupthink.

It's complex, but is it a lost cause?

Understanding exactly what is going on for everyone is impossible. What is possible is to facilitate risk analysis and management in a way that gives everyone the best chance of considering different perspectives and points of view. Great facilitation provides the group with a way of being thoughtful and considered before taking risks.

Working with people and their preferences

There are three main things that we can do to help people make more informed and rational decisions under uncertainty. These work for individuals and also for decision-making groups. In this section we will talk mainly about groups because this is the most complex and most common situation for people who are trying to make risk management work.

The three main things we can do are:

- Reframing
- Enabling conscious awareness
- Independent input.

Reframing

This idea originates from Kahneman and Tversky's original work on loss aversion but applies universally when trying to help people be as rational as possible when considering risk and making risk-based decisions.

The idea of the 'frame' is that it is the way an idea or concept is expressed – the words used, and the associated tone of voice, and non-verbal communication. Reframing then is using a different set of words and associated communication to convey the same idea.

Remember the cognitive bias loss aversion where we believe a solution that saves 40 per cent of lives is better than one that allows 50 per cent of the people to die.

Reframing the situation as 50 per cent of lives saved or 60 per cent of lives lost (exactly the same data) can trigger a different response. Try it – it's a really important skill for a facilitator of risk.

Enabling conscious awareness

This idea is also underpinned by some of Kahneman's work and described in his famous book – *Thinking, Fast and Slow*. If you haven't read it – please do. Slow thinking is what we need in risk analysis and management – thinking that is deliberate and not instinctive. This doesn't mean that it takes weeks and weeks to make a decision, but it does mean taking the time to think beyond your first, automatic, and maybe biased judgement. When facilitating risk, finding ways to give individuals and the group this thinking time is key, as is finding ways to bring attention to things you notice; for example, 'Did you notice how quickly you all seemed to agree on that point? What might be going on there?'

Independent input

At the most basic level, independent input from a range of people on the same question is a way of flushing out individual views and avoiding the pitfalls of groupthink. As we will discuss in Chapter 5, this is of massive value when coming to a consensus on the likelihood and size of impact of a risk.

But what's also interesting is who we ask. Across many societies we have learned to value the 'expert' view, but this is not rational if the 'expert' is biased.

In his book, *The Wisdom of Crowds*, James Surowiecki provides compelling evidence of how large numbers of people with some relevant knowledge are far better at estimating and deciding than experts. This is directly applicable to making risk management work, and through a variety of in-person and virtual techniques is really easy to facilitate.

Summary

People make decisions in risky and important situations and those decisions commit them, their families, their communities, their companies – often based on erroneous data.

This chapter has mentioned a number of ways that people are biased – and there are many other ways, too. But three approaches that the facilitator can adopt are really effective in interrupting automatic, often biased thought and bring the group to a better decision.

So having established these, we can now explore how they can be applied through the risk management process (Chapter 5), during in-person risk workshops (Chapter 6), and when working virtually – either fully remote or hybrid (Chapter 7).

Questions for reflection

1   What decisions have you made that in retrospect were biased?
2   How might you avoid repeating the problem?
3   Where have you seen individuals or groups tackling bias head-on? What did they do? How did it work? What would you do in that position?
4   How will what you've learned in this chapter change how you approach risk management?

References and further reading

Duke, A. (2020). *How to decide: Simple tools for making better choices.* Penguin Publishing Group.
Freud, S., & Strachey, J. (1989). *Beyond the pleasure principle.* Norton.

Hillson, D.A., & Murray-Webster, R. (2007). *Understanding and managing risk attitude* (2nd ed.). Gower.

Kahneman, D. (2011). *Thinking, fast and slow*. Farrar, Straus and Giroux.

LeDoux, J. (1996). *The emotional brain: The mysterious underpinnings of emotional life*. Simon and Schuster.

Stavros, J., & Torres, C. (2018). *Conversations worth having: Using appreciative inquiry to fuel productive and meaningful engagement*. Berrett-Koehler Publishers.

Surowiecki, J. (2004). *The wisdom of crowds*. Anchor.

Sustein, C. R., & Hastie, R. (2015). *Wiser: Getting beyond groupthink to make groups smarter*. Harvard Business Review Press.

To explore the structure of the brain in detail, we recommend the interactive 3D model at www.brainfacts.org/3d-brain

4 Why risk facilitation matters

Risk facilitation concerns all those skills we use when we make risk management work really well with other people. Risk facilitators get the best from risk processes, work with groups to manage risk within organisations, and run risk workshops effectively. If you do this, then you are acting as a risk facilitator, whatever your job title and whatever the proportion of your time it takes up.

What *exactly* does the term risk facilitator mean? The root of the word 'facile' comes from the Latin 'to make easy'. So a facilitator is someone who makes something easy. A risk facilitator is someone who makes risk management work as easily as possible. They bring energy and life to what can be a dull and pedantic process.

DOI: 10.4324/9781003245858-4

Unfortunately, energy and life are frequently absent in risk management. Too often we've found that risk registers are completed and then ignored. We've even found quotes such as "risk identification meetings are tedious and detailed" in reference books! While this may be a very common experience, we disagree that this has to be so. Bringing risk management to life by engaging people is possible. We'll explain how you can do it and the difference it makes. We'll share stories from people who have brought risk alive inside their organisation later in this chapter.

What is facilitation?

Facilitation is growing as a profession in its own right and as a key skill for organisations. Why is this so? We're moving from an era of command-and-control into one where we need to get things done through other people, often without any line management authority. This is a challenge faced by risk facilitators. They need to get people across their organisation to take risks seriously and to take action as a result.

Facilitation is not just a set of skills. It's also an attitude of mind, whereby we choose to do what we can to make it as easy as possible for people to achieve their outcomes. There is quite a body of information about facilitation. You can find some references at the end of this chapter. For an overview of facilitation of risk workshops, see Chapter 6, and for an overview of making risk management work in virtual settings, whether fully remote or hybrid, see Chapter 7.

Facilitators need a whole set of skills. These include being able to:

1 *Work with large and increasingly diverse groups:* new facilitators might just work within their own teams. As they develop their skills, they will work with larger groups of people from across their organisation and from all levels of the hierarchy.

Those who work with global teams, or across organisations, need to be able to handle major cultural differences across group members.

2 *Manage their own state and that of the groups they work with:* this will encourage people to tackle risks and take action. If the facilitator is tired and not interested, the group will be affected. If the group is tired and bored, the facilitator has little chance of stimulating ideas or gaining commitment to action from them. So facilitators need to have a range of tools and techniques up their sleeve to make sure that they are as effective as possible, both for themselves and for their groups. They need to be able to shift the group to a state appropriate for each task. For example, a state of positive and creative anticipation is useful when searching for opportunities. If a group is flagging, they probably won't come up with many! There is more on how to handle this in Chapter 6.

3 *Work in person or virtually:* those working together to manage risk might be together in person in one place, spread apart geographically, or indeed a hybrid mix of the two. There are particular skills in getting the best out of a group where at least part of the group is remote. Facilitators need skills both in dealing with and using technology and also knowing how to work without the visual clues of body language and the deep relationships that people can develop when together in person. Virtual groups may be mixed culturally or across time zones, adding even more complexity to the facilitator's job. Chapter 7 is focused on the extra challenges this brings.

4 *Deal with conflict:* people will have different viewpoints, particularly about the importance and impact of risks. This leads to disagreements and even tension. Conflict of this sort should be welcomed rather than frowned upon. With such 'task conflict', it's good to listen to all the different viewpoints of individuals in a group in order to build up a complete picture while keeping tension to a minimum. Relationship conflict is a different matter. This destructive form of conflict needs to be sorted out

quickly before it destroys the trust and commitment of each person to the group. For more practical ideas on how to do this, see Chapter 6.

5 *Be familiar with a wide range of facilitation tools and techniques:* facilitators need to have a range of tools and techniques at their fingertips and to be able to adapt these to meet the needs of the group they're working with. For example, a facilitator might start to gather information from a group by asking each person to give their input out loud. If someone starts to criticise ideas, the facilitator should change the way they gather information to something more anonymous in order to encourage people to contribute. Some ideas for this might include writing ideas on sticky notes (in person) or using an anonymous collaboration tool (virtual). There is a wide range of media options for those using technology to support virtual teams. Virtual risk facilitators need to know which options work well and in what circumstances.

6 *Sustain participation:* the best risk facilitators keep risk alive, bringing people with them throughout the whole risk management process. With many less experienced facilitators, this does not happen. Any initial enthusiasm fizzles out, making people much less likely to bother identifying and dealing with new risks that arise.

7 *Guide groups to outcomes:* facilitators need to be focused on the outcome for their group. They need to guide the group using a variety of approaches to ensure that the outcome is met, tasks are completed, and actions are agreed.

Facilitators need to be skilled in managing group dynamics and processes as well as the skills listed above. While neutral facilitators lead groups to outcomes, this doesn't mean they deal with the actual content of discussions. It really helps to keep the content and the process separate. A helpful way to think of this uses a hamburger analogy for a facilitated session.

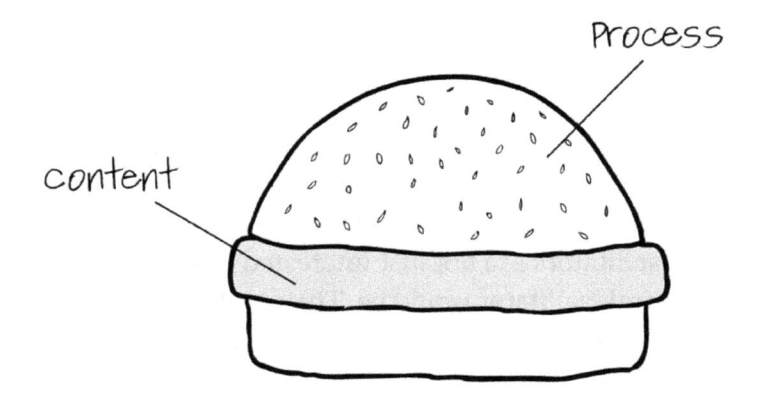

[Diagram: A burger illustration with "content" labeling the patty and "Process" labeling the bun.]

The burger represents the *content* of the facilitated session, the 'meat'. The bread bun around the burger represents how and when things happen to the content, that is, the *process*. When acting as a facilitator, you need to stay neutral and 'vegetarian' by staying out of other people's content and concentrating on the process that brings the best result for the group. Simple, isn't it?

However, it's not quite this straightforward for a risk facilitator. First, you require a thorough understanding of risk management as laid out in Chapter 2. Second, you need to understand each step of the risk process and how to facilitate it from Chapter 5. Third, you have to be able to challenge the risks that people come up with. Here are some reasons why risk facilitators need to challenge their groups:

- To separate out issues (where there is no uncertainly) from real risks (which are uncertain)
- To make sure that causes of risk are separated from risk events and from the effects of those risks
- To challenge group dynamics and biases that may be leading to skewed perspectives.

Unless you facilitate risk for your own team or project, you are unlikely to own the risks. You need to make sure that ownership of risk stays with the people responsible for their areas. That's one of the ways of keeping risk alive.

So, we propose a slight addition to the hamburger model for risk facilitators, adding some lettuce and slices of tomato to represent your knowledge of risk management and your ability to challenge risks. Risk facilitators are not just interested in the facilitation process as a neutral facilitator would be. They're also interested in making sure that people understand risk and that they have formulated their risks in a way that is helpful.

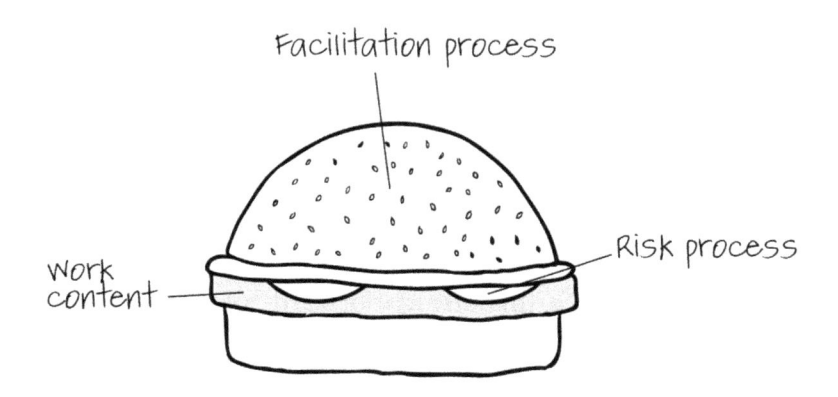

Penny interviewed John for this book. Here's his take on the role of risk facilitator:

> John has been facilitating risk management for years. Why? "I suppose I have a masochistic streak", he laughs. "Risk is often an area no one else is interested in doing as they don't want to be labelled as negative". John's record of delivery shows he's quite the opposite. What are his top tips for making risk management work? "Do what it takes to get people enthused. Get momentum and keep it real. Add in structure and clear thinking, while keeping it fun. Be careful with tools. They can get in the way *if* they get too complex. I like yellow stickies!" Why does John think that a risk facilitator

is so valuable? "Risk management works best when you have someone who is detached *from* the risks and who has an absolute handle on the process."

Where in the organisation might you find a risk facilitator?

'Risk facilitator' is a role unlikely to be listed on an organisation chart. But those who make risk work as easy as possible within an organisation *are* risk facilitators. Where in the organisation might we find such people? Well, there are many areas. These include business continuity, financial, health and safety, environmental, security, organisational change, or risk, to name just a few in larger organisations, and director, manager, or, in fact, anyone in a smaller organisation!

One common area to find people doing risk facilitation is in project management. Project managers can be interested in risks to their own project, as well as helping other people with risks on their projects. Business analysts are particularly interested in risks to requirements. Sometimes people inside project support offices look after the facilitation of risk across their organisation.

Other risk facilitators can be found in governance roles. Increasingly, facilitators are found within specialist risk departments at corporate level.

How much time do risk facilitators spend actually facilitating risk? Well, this can vary enormously from almost nothing, perhaps just a few hours a year, to almost all of their time.

Risk facilitators may operate as internal consultants inside organisations. This is a role that Penny played for many years inside Mars Inc. as an internal consultant in the Effective Business Change team. One aspect of her role was to facilitate risk workshops.

Another was to develop the facilitation capabilities of the company. There are advantages for risk facilitators who are internal consultants: they know the culture of the organisation. They know what works, and they're likely to be well aware of common issues. The disadvantage though is that it can be easy to become caught up in internal politics. It can be difficult to remain as neutral as someone external.

Later, Penny left Mars to become an external consultant. That's another place where you can find risk facilitators. External consultants give you several advantages. They are more neutral than internal consultants. They specialise in risk and have lots of experience. (It's rare, though, for consultants to combine expertise in risk along with practical experience and skills in facilitation. This is why we have written this book to share our skills and experience across both areas.)

External experts with the right skills will have a wide view across different companies so they can see how you're doing in comparison to other companies. They can ask the 'dumb' questions that people inside the organisation would find difficult to ask. Of course, 'dumb' questions, in reality, may be clever questions and very helpful. External consultants are outside of the politics of the organisation in many respects.

What are some of the disadvantages of using external experts? Well, they may not know your organisational culture. They certainly won't have had the time that an internal consultant has had to pick up the culture and learn to work with it. They are also likely to cost more in the short term, so any additional expense upfront will need to be justified.

Here are three stories to show how effective risk facilitators can be inside organisations. Vivien, Chris, and Anna's stories highlight different aspects of how to make risk management work.

Vivien's story

History

Vivien works in risk within a major pharmaceutical company. A few years ago, the company had a special tool used to capture and track risks. To quote Vivien, "the very nature of the tool killed energy and creativity." This software tool needed a team of full-time experts whose sole job was to make sure that the tool was being used correctly and risks were added to it. However, these experts were rather out of touch with the main business. Managers would be trained on the tool, but not in how to facilitate risk. They were expected to enter data into the tool as part of their job. Risk management wasn't really alive. The tool wasn't being used on an ongoing basis. People felt that they had to put data into the tool and once that was done, the job was done. But it wasn't.

Things start to change

Since Vivien became involved, there have been many changes. Now both the purpose and objectives of risk management are very clear, and there are formal criteria for what should be included. The old, complicated software tool has gone and been replaced with simple templates. Risk is not just a focus for the risk team but is part of the role of all managers. Instead of a specialist risk team, there is a whole network of risk people who have been trained in facilitation as well as risk. These risk facilitators ensure the 'process' works well, challenging facts, and bringing energy to the risk management process.

Each category of risk has a global risk owner who oversees that category as part of their role. The 'owners' ensure that risk is monitored and that appropriate actions are progressed. They are based in different business functions. The risk facilitators meet – normally virtually – to develop a central risk picture from across the business. Vivien provides ideas and risk themes to support their work. They run risk workshops to inspire the rest of the organisation.

The key thing about this change was to change the culture of the organisation from turning a handle on a risk 'sausage machine' to keeping risk management alive.

The results

How does risk management work now? Key performance indicators for risk are in place and reported against with information feeding up to the most senior levels of the organisation from different parts of the organisation globally. The board has a clear and comprehensive risk picture that is built up from reports from around the world. There is a network of people involved. There is an ongoing process, a very simple process, but it does enable people's buy-in and engagement. It keeps people accountable for their actions. The whole process is pragmatic and focuses on action rather than dictating precise steps to follow. Workshops are a key part, helping to embed risk into people's roles and responsibilities. The major risks to the organisation are updated regularly.

Lessons from Vivien on how to make risk management work

It's very easy when facilitating risk management to be unclear about what you're doing and why. This tends to leave people drowning in the detail. Everyone involved needs to know where their roles and responsibilities begin and end.

Vivien suggests that we should be really clear about who is accountable for each risk. "Make sure there is ownership. When risks overlap areas, you'll need to choose whether to duplicate the ownership, or to align and dovetail the ownership."

Vivien feels that many organisations go straight to using a tool, especially when they have a lot of information. While tools can be helpful, she advises against using them at the very first stage.

The culture of the organisation is key to success. To make risk management work, you need people who are committed to identifying and responding to risk, not those who will only give lip service. You don't want 'handle-turners' to use the sausage machine metaphor again. Risk should be an integrated part of strategic and business performance planning.

Vivien told me more about the role of the risk facilitator, which has been so successful in her organisation. The risk facilitator needs to have creative skills, especially when it comes to working with groups. They need to be aware of a range of facilitation methods and be able to use those methods effectively. They need to be able to work both in a detailed way and at a big picture/high level to communicate better with the senior managers. The risk facilitator has to be able to challenge people at all levels of the organisation in order to be effective. This is crucial to success. Many people will portray issues as risks or try to avoid action. The risk facilitator needs to see connections between different things and spot risks that exacerbate each other across areas. While they might not manage projects as such, they'll find project management skills such as action tracking and following up to be very helpful. When working with senior people, their personal reputation and credibility is especially important as they need to be trusted. It's important, too, that risk facilitators understand the players and the politics involved.

Vivien was able to do all of these things herself and inspire others, which ultimately led to her success.

Chris's story

History

Chris works in a risk and regulatory role within a small, innovative start-up company dealing with financial technology (FinTech).

The culture of the company, focused on innovative solutions and fast growth, does not naturally warm to a process of considering things that potentially may happen. Leaders are much more used to taking a chance and responding to whatever comes their way. Chris's attempts to get leaders focused on identifying risks were really difficult. People were polite, but their hearts were not in it.

But this is FinTech, and the products that are being developed need to be approved by the financial regulator – in this case in a country that is well known for its willingness to take legal action to settle disputes. Ignoring risk and just taking the chance is not going to enable the company to get the licences it needs – something has to change.

Things start to change

Things started to change when Chris stopped trying to get his colleagues to identify risks starting with a blank sheet of paper. He decided to try all sorts of different techniques to stimulate conversation about things that may occur in future without actually using the 'R' word (risk!).

One approach that the team really engaged with was creating multiple potential future scenarios for the company and then discussing what would have had to happen for each of these scenarios to have occurred. This stimulated conversation about opportunities that would need to be seized and threats that would need to be avoided if possible. Chris set up the sessions with lots of opportunities for people to talk, to draw, and to debate. Rather than Chris trying to control a risk process, instead he set up the conditions for the group to naturally explore risks in their own way.

Chris kept all the hand-drawn visuals from the session and three months later reconvened a session to revisit these and refresh the story. This worked well and became part of the quarterly process for the leadership team.

The results

The results were very successful. The group engaged in a process that meant something to them; then Chris could translate their work into the formats that were needed by regulators and other assurance bodies. The leadership team was not stifled by a process they did not value, but they engaged in a different process that gave the same outputs.

Lessons from Chris on how to make risk management work

Chris says, "As long as you know the end point you need, there are many ways of getting there, research different techniques and try them out with your group".

As with Vivien's story, the culture of the organisation is key to success. You have to know your stakeholders and design something that will engage them. Only if you engage stakeholders will they identify, own, and manage risk.

Chris also really stresses the importance of the hamburger with the lettuce and tomato for risk facilitators. The facilitator must be neutral in that they really must not have a view on the content, but they must be knowledgeable in the risk process and how to get a quality, unbiased output from a group.

The key advice from Chris though is to be creative – research different things and try them.

Anna's story

History

Anna works for a large IT company in a programme management office (PMO). The company has a very longstanding and well-developed risk management process that is thought through, properly documented, and supported by a sophisticated tool. If you asked people in the organisation, they would say that risk management was very important: 'Just look at our process and tool!' In reality there was mass 'lip service' and the extent and quality of implementation was very poor. Anna believed in the process and was frustrated with the response from her project manager, programme manager, and senior management colleagues. What could she do to unlock the potential of the process?

Things start to change

Anna runs a regular risk governance meeting. The key people used either to attend reluctantly or not at all. The meeting process was well established and formulaic, with a detailed review of each project and the risks and risk responses within it. Anna decided to change this and to facilitate the next meeting in a different way. She circulated the information in advance (as usual) but asked each person to prepare a two minute summary of what they were most worried about with their work at the current time. They were not constrained by reading the risks from the register. Rather they were encouraged to offer their personal summary of what was most risky about the work, and why. The energy in the room was greatly improved in that meeting, and new risks were identified and new perspectives gained. The next month the same happened. It only took 3 to 4 months for the meetings to be transformed into interesting discussions that all the key people attended without exception. Anna was able to challenge more and facilitate discussions that just did not happen in the past.

The results

The real test came when Anna was away from work with an illness for 3 months. On her return she was delighted to see that the process had continued during her absence. Without her, people were regularly identifying, prioritising, and managing risks. Governance was effective in communicating shared risky areas and escalating those risks that needed senior management action. Anna's senior manager commented, "the difference between Anna and other risk specialists is that she listens to us, understands what we are saying, and doesn't beat us up with the minutiae of the process. We trust her to add value to any of our management meetings." Anna said, "I learned to let some things go, but I asked lots of questions so I understood the situation, then I could make the information fit into the official process back at my desk later. That way all the arguments about the process stopping the work getting done ended."

Lessons from Anna on how to make risk management work

Anna found a way to step out of the role of policeman and into the role of facilitator. She didn't abandon her strong beliefs in the process itself. Nevertheless, she did abandon trying to get the managers in her area to share her enthusiasm and belief. Instead, she focused on what was on their minds and took the detailed work of complying with the process through quality outputs away from them. Over time, they learned to do a good job themselves. This was a major step forward.

The development path for risk facilitators

If you want to develop your risk facilitation skills, how can you do this? How can you help your organisation develop an effective risk management culture?

1 *Advice for individual risk facilitators*

How can you develop as your own skills as a risk facilitator? Have a go in a small way once you understand risk management as laid out in Chapter 2. Many people learn how to work with groups through years of experience. However, we've found the *quickest* way to develop the specific skills of a risk facilitator is through a mixture of both training and support from risk facilitation experts *at the same time* as putting them into practice in the workplace. You can find out more about workshops to support you further, as well as assessing your skills as a risk facilitator, at www.makingriskwork.com.

To stretch your skills beyond your comfort zone, we suggest that you co-facilitate with somebody else who is more experienced than you. That way you can build up your experience. Later, you will be able to facilitate on your own at that level. Build up to larger groups, more diverse groups, and groups where the stakes are higher, the risks are larger, and/or the people are more senior. Use the later chapters of this book for ideas you can try.

It's well worth working with others as you develop. For example, Ruth and Penny worked with a team of risk specialists within an organisation to help them develop their skills as facilitators of the risk management process. They not only share ideas and support each other but co-facilitate sessions together to build their skills and confidence and to learn from each other's feedback.

We would strongly advise that individual risk facilitators find others to support them through their development process.

2 *Advice for organisations*

The development path for organisations is less clear.

How can you start to develop an organisation's approach? The first step is to make sure that people understand the value of the risk facilitator. Often administrators, risk coordinators, or even people who handle the tools are given the role, as opposed to skilled risk facilitators. The difference that skilled facilitators make is clear from Vivien, Chris, and Anna's stories.

A key step is to define the role of the risk facilitator formally in a job description or 'person specification' that people can be selected against. Once the role is accepted as necessary by senior leaders, others begin to accept that facilitation of risk management is crucial.

Summary

Some key pointers for risk facilitators are:

1 They have a range of special skills
2 They need to manage both the facilitation and the risk management process, but stay out of the content; they need to be vegetarian (remember the hamburger model!)
3 You can find them almost anywhere within organisations, as risk facilitation is a role and not a job
4 They can develop their skills as individuals; we've shown a range of competencies to focus on and how

5 A supportive organisational culture is required
6 They can make a big difference.

Through Vivien, Chris, and Anna's stories you can see how these play out in real life. In the next chapter, we'll look at how you can facilitate the risk process in different organisational settings and *contexts*.

Questions for reflection

1 How much of your role is risk facilitation?
2 Using the hamburger model, consider how you facilitate risk management. How 'vegetarian' are you? What will you change going forward?
3 What did you learn from Vivien, Chris, and Anna?
4 How will you develop your skills in risk facilitation going forward, and who will you ask to support you as you progress?

Reference and further reading

International Association of Facilitators (IAF). (2021). *IAF core competencies*. Retrieved February 4, 2022, from www.iaf-world.org/site/professional/core-competencies

5 Facilitating the risk management process

So far, we've explored the principles of risk management in Chapter 2, looked at the things that bias people's perception of risk in Chapter 3, and examined the role of the facilitator in Chapter 4. Now we put these together to cover how you can facilitate the risk management process.

Remember the hamburger model Chapter 2? Great facilitators stay vegetarian: they don't get involved with the 'meat' that represents the actual risks. But risk facilitators do need to have the lettuce and tomato, as well as the bun – they are responsible for making it easy for the group to implement really effective risk management. To do that they need to be well versed in risk management principles, tools, and techniques, as well as be able to demonstrate all the qualities of a great facilitator.

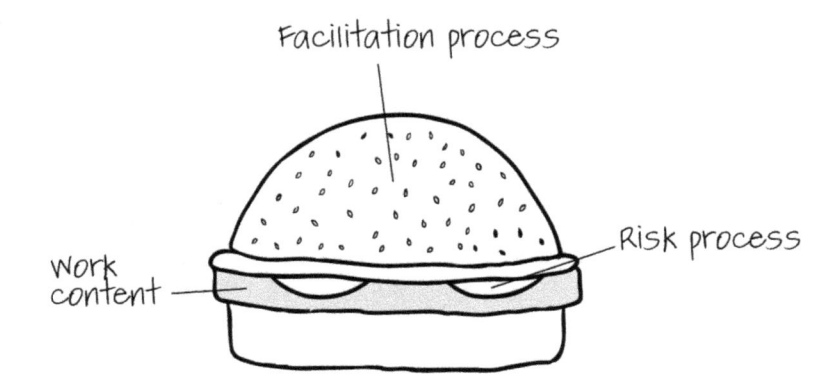

DOI: 10.4324/9781003245858-5

Not just workshops

Many people will associate a risk facilitator with 'risk workshops'. The term 'risk workshop' is typically used to describe a situation where a group of people come together, either in person or virtually, to work through part of the risk management process. Facilitating workshops is a crucial part of the work – but not the only part.

The whole of the risk management process, from understanding objectives and tolerances through to monitoring and control, can be facilitated with great effect.

Great risk facilitators know how to engage the team and achieve the right balance between work done *in* workshops (whether in person or virtual), and work done *out* of workshops. The right balance means only using workshops for work that requires creativity, collaboration, and commitment or using workshops for surfacing and dealing with conflict. It is better to do the work that requires detailed analysis in another way. Many people have told both Ruth and Penny that their experience of risk workshops is often dull and boring. However, we also know from feedback that workshops *can* be inspirational sessions that really get the team thinking and working together on risk. They can kick-start a focus on risk management that endures.

So, how can we all design our risk facilitation to inspire people, rather than put them to sleep? From our experience, there are three general 'rules'. These three rules are explained, followed by some examples of tried and tested ways to get the work done.

General rules for risk facilitation

Engage the right people at the right time

It's really important that you learn who the stakeholders are and where those stakeholders are coming from in terms of objectives, power, interest, and attitude. This will start with your 'client' for the work. If a formal stakeholder analysis exists, get hold of it and verify the information. If not, ask lots of questions and make sure you have a good understanding of who is involved and what their perspectives on risk are likely to be before you start to engage them. You also need to know some other practical things about stakeholders, such as where they're located, their national cultural backgrounds, their past experiences of risk management, whether they have funding to travel, and so on. The more you know at the start, the easier it will be as you progress.

Energise, and keep the energy

Doing risk management well is detailed and often difficult work. This means it can so easily become laborious and frustrating. As facilitator, you need to take responsibility for helping the team find, as well as maintain, focus and energy.

Doing this, in turn, can take a lot of your energy as you work on creating the right group dynamic as well as keeping focused enough to be able to challenge. Our own experience is that helping the group to become positively energised and to keep that energy becomes much easier the more experienced you become with implementing the risk management process. Once these skills become second nature to you, it will free you up to focus on the group rather than the process and the different ways to keep the group engaged and participating.

Challenge, but stay vegetarian

This can be tricky. Your quest as a risk facilitator is to uphold the quality of the risk management process. You need to tease out risks from issues, challenge preconceived views, see if there is systematic bias emerging, or offer alternative strategies when response planning. Your challenge is to refrain from offering your own perceptions of the nature and extent of risks or your opinions about priorities and responses. *The group own the risks.* You are there simply to ease the process to define and manage those risks. So, keep your challenges vegetarian and things should be okay.

What to do, and ways to do it

In this section we break the risk management process down into separate steps, highlighting the questions that each step of the process must answer, and the outputs that are needed. We also outline some different ways that we have facilitated each step of the process ourselves. These are offered as tried and tested examples. There will, of course, be many other ways to achieve successful outcomes.

Governance of the risk management process

Governance must underpin all the process steps. What does this mean? In this context, governance simply means that the senior leaders of the organisation must put in place arrangements to monitor progress, to escalate or delegate decisions to the right level of management, and to provide a decision-making regime that gets best use from the risk management process. By doing this, senior leaders begin to show their support for risk management.

In the most successful organisations, senior leaders provide a supportive culture. Here the nature of uncertainty and risk are understood, and the management of uncertainties that matter most is measurably efficient *and* effective.

Step 1: initiating risk management or 'how much risk can we tolerate?'

Questions to be answered	Outputs
Who are the stakeholders? What are their objectives? How will these be measured? Who will judge? Which objectives take (relative) priority when things get tough? How much risk to these objectives are you prepared to tolerate? What process will you use to manage the risks to objectives?	SMART (specific, measurable, agreed, realistic, and timed) statements of objectives in priority order, with defined impact scales and risk tolerances for each objective. Risk management plan, including a stakeholder analysis and engagement plan, and defined and agreed probability and impact scales.

Tried and tested tips

- If it is possible to get the key people together easily, then using a couple of hours for an in-person workshop can be a really effective way to answer the questions. Take the follow-up work offline: tidying the input and presenting back SMART statements of objectives along with a draft risk management plan.
- If people are spread out geographically but know one another and the work to be done, you can use a virtual meeting (fully remote or hybrid – see Chapter 7) with a shared screen where you can share information in real time. As before, tidy the input and present back SMART statements of objectives along with a draft risk management plan offline.
- If people are geographically spread out and don't know one another well, you can work with one or two senior people to prepare a draft set of objectives and risk management plan. After this you can take the time to share this with the other stakeholders in one-to-one calls, inviting them to share any different perspectives they have. When you have verified (or otherwise) the draft objectives and plan, you can then decide how to progress. When there are different perspectives – and there usually are – you can bring people together to resolve any differences at the start of the next stage.

Step 2: identifying and describing individual risks or 'what's risky and why?'

Questions to be answered	Outputs
What are the potential opportunities – things that might occur that would improve the achievement of objectives?	List of risks, described well, separating causes, from risk events from effects (as described in Chapter 2)
What are the potential problems –things that might occur that would harm the achievement of objectives?	
Who is the best owner for each risk?	

This is work that requires:

- Creativity, to open up the mind to what may occur
- Detailed work – to explore the relationships between causes, risk events, and effects and to write clear risk descriptions.

Tried and tested tips

- If you can get the group together in person and you have good experience in facilitating risk management, you may well be able to facilitate the creative and detailed aspects of this step together, that is, by taking the output from the group and turning it into clear and complete descriptions during the workshop. Ruth has done this with groups of more than 20 people and captured the risk descriptions on flip charts. These were pasted up around the room. An alternative to this is to capture the output straight into a table of risks on a laptop projected onto a wall. This output will be ready to send out electronically immediately after the workshop.
- If you can get the group together in person but have less time together, or are less experienced, it can be more useful to facilitate a creative session with the group first, capturing the outputs in any way you wish. Then take them offline to create detailed risk descriptions for the risk register. Share this work with the group to validate and/or change the draft descriptions at a later time. This way usual works best – it can be boring to watch someone typing!
- If it is difficult to get the group together in person, try using a remote brainstorming technique to get each individual to identify risks and then share the output with the whole group to continue the creative process. Modern technology has enabled a number of innovative solutions to this sort of task. You, as facilitator, can take time during this process to make sure causes, risk events, and effects are clearly articulated so that the output is clear and everyone agrees with it.

Potential problems and potential opportunities

Whatever approach you use for risk identification, we have found that some experienced groups are able to deal with the identification of potential opportunities and potential problems in the same process. In contrast, less experienced groups often struggle with this. Our experience is that it is useful to focus on identifying potential opportunities *first*. When no more can be identified, then move to the threats. One of our colleagues also makes great use of physical prompts such as issuing 'rose-tinted spectacles' to people to help them think positively, or by putting the ideas behind De Bono's *Six Thinking Hats*, for example the yellow hat for optimism, to great use. Sensing when such prompts can help a group progress is a key skill of a successful facilitator.

Step 3: prioritising individual risks or 'how much does each risk matter?'

Questions to be answered	Outputs
How would the identified risks impact objectives if they occurred? What is the chance that each risk would have that impact on objectives?	Register of unmanaged risks populated, prioritised, challenged, and communicated to relevant stakeholders

This is the step in the process that is the most subjective and the most open to human bias. It's the step that can really sap energy if the group feels that their effort is not leading to good outcomes. Facilitators can make a huge difference here. In addition to the well-described risks from the previous step, you need to have the probability and impact scales already agreed. Remember that these scales articulate what matters most and how much risk can be tolerated.

Tried and tested tips

- If you decide to facilitate this step of the process in an in-person workshop, the key thing is to keep the assessment as objective as possible, while keeping everyone involved. We strongly advise *not* to have the whole group of people assessing probability and impact together. This takes too long and is one sure way of supporting the reputation of risk management being tedious and dull! It doesn't have to be like this.
- One idea is to separate the assessment of impact from the assessment of probability. For example, if risks are written on flip charts pasted around the room, you can have the group on their feet, starting at different places and walking around. They can add their assessment of impact beside each risk and note differences in opinion from other group members with arrows (up or down from the first assessment). The process can then be repeated for the assessment of probability. To make this work well, especially with an inexperienced group, you need clear rules for framing the questions to be answered. Agree on these and put them on the wall.

The questions that this step of the process must answer are:

- If this risk occurred, how big would the impact be (as per the defined impact scales)
- What is the chance that this risk might occur (as per the defined probability scales)?

Another technique in a workshop setting is to break up the group into smaller teams, with each team considering a proportion of the defined risks. The output from each smaller team can then be consolidated in a visual way and challenged by the other teams afterwards. At this stage any systematic bias can be challenged and dealt with. If you are using this technique, it's good to plan in some time for you as facilitator to consolidate the output. Ruth's experience facilitating risk workshops is that she always plans to do a consolidating task over lunchtime in order to keep the process moving. (You get used to taking your food and drink when the group is working!) An alternative, of course, is to work on prioritising risks in an afternoon session, consolidate overnight, then challenge the following morning.

Although typically this step is done in an in-person workshop, we argue that this is not actually the best way. A virtual technique is much better at getting each individual stakeholder's perspective in the first instance. The output can then be pulled together by the facilitator remotely and shared – either virtually again or at the start of an in-person session.

Think again how workshops are used

In our experience, most groups seem to use workshops to facilitate every step of the process up to this point: to set objectives and the scales for prioritisation, to identify and describe risks, and to prioritise them. After this the group is typically out of time or out of energy to do more. For this reason, we would encourage everyone to think about doing the work up to this point in the process differently: for example, using separate short workshops if the geography allows or using virtual techniques to get to the point where all stakeholders have had their input on the risks and their priorities. After this you can bring the group together for challenge, consolidation, and response planning. Varying the way you achieve the outcomes of this step of the process also prevents stagnation and boredom.

Step 4: assessing overall riskiness, or 'how risky is this situation?'

Questions to be answered	Outputs
Which risks are mutually exclusive?	Visualisation of the combined risk impact on objectives
Which risks are correlated?	Note: this can be done qualitatively or quantitatively depending on the needs of the organisation
What is the combined impact of all risks on objectives?	

This step of the process is often missed out, which then leaves a big gap in the value of the risk management process. An overall map of the risks to objectives is a useful way to support assessment of the overall riskiness of the situation. Mutually exclusive risks must be identified, so that if risk A occurs, risk B cannot. Similarly, correlated risks must be identified, so that if risk C occurs then risk D must also.

Tried and tested tips

- This step works best with a small number of people, ideally just the risk owners, coming together in person to create the overall map of risks. If it's not possible to get the right people physically together, the same effect can be created by the facilitator carrying out a series of interviews then piecing together the overall picture. However, this is more difficult to do well and takes a lot more time. The facilitator must ensure there is understanding of how each of the risks relate to each other as this is a necessary first step for subsequent qualitative or quantitative analysis.
- Most organisations visualise the complete set of risks in a situation on some sort of grid, typically called a probability/impact grid, a risk assessment matrix, or a heat map. The beauty of such visualisations is that they can be both created and kept up to date easily. There are many different ways of creating such visualisations. We strongly recommend using a method where you can clearly visualise both potential problems and potential opportunities. Some organisations do not do any further analysis of the combined impact of all risks on objectives.
- If your organisation uses a more sophisticated, quantitative technique, building probabilistic models and analysing these statistically, then our top tips for getting quality output are as follows. First, be sure that the 'right' stakeholders are involved – those with relevant experience and those who know what historical data is relevant and available. Second, be sure that the team has at least one member who understands the statistics involved and can help the team avoid building anomalies into the model. The

effect of the central limit theorem or nodal bias can cause particular problems – someone in the team must understand how to overcome such problems. Third, make sure there is a transparent link between the risk register and the risk model, that is, that the range estimates and judgements of probability have taken into account the risks that have been identified. Finally, ensure the model and the outputs from the simulations have a 'sanity check' by challenging the underlying assumptions of the model.

Step 5: responding to risks, or 'what action shall we take?'

Questions to be answered	Outputs
Can the risks be tolerated and left unmanaged?	Updated risk register to include response plans and expected residual risk, and identification of any secondary risks.
If not, what is the response to each risk that gives best value for money/effort?	Updated plans.
Who will do what to manage the risk?	
What risk is expected to remain if response plans are effective? (residual risk)	
What other risks might be caused by the response plan? (Secondary risks)	

Chapter 2 outlined the options open to risk owners: take the risk, prepare a plan B, treat the risk, share (not transfer) the risk, or make it certain. Most typically this work is not done in meetings or workshops because:

- The workshop has been used for earlier stages in the process and the team have run out of time and/or steam
- The work of response planning is delegated to risk owners.

This can be the start of the potential decline in attention given to risk management, the slide from the energised workshop to the stagnant process. What can be done differently?

Tried and tested tips

- There are big benefits in using the group who assessed the overall riskiness of the work in the previous step to plan responses. They can then share their output with the wider group of stakeholders at a later stage. The benefits of this approach arise because the group is concentrating not just on individual risks, but the combined effect of risks to objectives. Keeping this concentration ensures responses focused on the defined risk tolerance for the work and a sense of value, that is, is the action you take to respond to a risk worth it?
- In particularly complex, risky situations, you could consider using what is known as a scenario planning technique. Scenario planning is completely reliant on great facilitation. Originally a strategic planning technique, it can be used to get groups of people to envisage possible alternative futures and then to plan what actions are needed to secure the desired future outcome. Ruth has used this technique with groups who knew what they wanted to achieve, but where the route to achieving that was complex because of many competing threats and opportunities. Creating a setting where people can tell stories and draw visual depictions of action plans to respond to the risks is a key part of making scenario planning work well.
- Another option is to invite different 'experts' to share their experiences and suggest response options. People who are not stakeholders for the work, but who have experience of doing similar things, are ideal contributors. They are not emotionally attached to the work and achievement of objectives and can often cut through bias by challenging perspectives. In our experience, the facilitator's job in such a situation is to get the best out of the visitors while at the same time ensuring that the team

can 'hear' the advice. It goes without saying that this option requires a setting where people are open and willing to consider different perspectives.
- Ultimately, response plans need to be 'worth it', that is, the investment in the response plan can be justified in terms of the reduction in residual risk. We have found that facilitators can be of great worth here by providing challenge to make sure that the investment in risk management is demonstrably beneficial.

Step 6: keeping the process alive, or 'what's the current status?'

Questions to be answered	Outputs
What has changed since the last review?	Updated risk register

Tried and tested tips

You may recall from Vivien, Chris, and Anna's stories in Chapter 4 that they had found a way of keeping the process alive. Unfortunately, this is rare.

If the rest of the process has gone well, the challenge at this stage is how to track and manage a large number of well-described and assessed risks.

This is a question posed by one of our clients.

> "I am hoping you will be able to offer some advice on conducting risk review meetings and using the time effectively. We recently carried out a risk facilitation session with the senior management team to generate a new risk register. We used a lot of the interactive techniques you taught us, and the response was excellent.
>
> One of the problems, however, is that we now have a huge number of risks to manage! We have two registers – one

for the business that contains mainly reputation, health and safety, and people risks. We have 63 risks on this risk register and reviews take place quarterly. The second register is the 'Programme' register that has 156 risks and contains commercial, delivery, and programme delivery risks. Reviews take place monthly. Both registers have a good mix of threats and opportunities.

How do we review these effectively? Do we need to focus attention only on the top priority risks? I did this at the last programme review, and it took 3 hours! We just about managed this, but it was a painful and slow process, and I was conscious of 130 others that we didn't even touch on. After the meeting I sent out a filtered version to the owners of lower priority risks that we didn't get round to reviewing and only one of the ten got back to me. The only other thing I could do is set up further 1:1s, but some owners have 20+ risks on the register and are unlikely to commit to another meeting every month on the back of the group 3-hour meeting. This is very time consuming for me as well, but I'm worried that after all the good work that has gone in to identifying all these risks nothing will change because nobody is reviewing them!

I know it's difficult and it's the behaviours that need to change but any suggestions or tips you have on how I could improve on this would be much appreciated."

Our response was as follows:

> "First – the very worst outcome here is that risks on your list are seen as *your* risks and the review process as *your* review. This can result in the managers involved feeling it's a chore and they're doing you a favour.
> Second – I worry about only reviewing the top risks (that is, the most likely, biggest impact). It is critical to keep an eye on

low probability/high impact risks as a minimum as these are often the ones that become real issues.

Some ideas to try are:

- You could devise a process where each risk owner comes to the review with a short exception report about their risks, that is, which ones have been worked on, which ones they're most worried about (threats), or enthusiastic about (opportunities), ones where – in their view – the priority has changed since last time, and, most importantly, the ones where they need help to manage them from elsewhere. I'm not sure how many risk owners there are, but if everyone had a 10-minute slot this would be doable. Everyone would learn from listening to their colleagues; for example, you could start to get information about common responses/solutions. You could even capture the content and then update the risk register offline. They could present their information any way they liked, as long as it covered the ground.
- Tell them that you want to make the time you have together in person as rich as possible – so ask people to give you an update offline before the meeting (using the same format as described above). You can then bring the risks that are most noteworthy to the meeting for discussion. This way the meeting doesn't get bogged down in boring reporting. Needless to say, this relies on an investment in time ahead of the meeting, but it would have a pay-off in terms of the actual quality of the meeting process and output.
- If you can't split the risk register by risk owner, you could divide it by line manager or by risk 'type', that is commercial, delivery, programme delivery, and so on. However, with this suggestion, it may be more difficult to get one person to take ownership of the feedback provided.
- To show this visually, you could have a traffic light system, along the following lines:

Red: a concern (either because risk is not being managed, it hasn't been reviewed for 3 months or more, or it doesn't have an agreed response)

Amber: a minor concern (not managed, hasn't been reviewed for 2 months, or is out of date in some way)

Green: only achieved if the risk has been reviewed in the last month and has an agreed response plan that is under control (even if the response is simply to accept and monitor).

- It's also really important to remain focused on the overall objectives for the work and the amount of risk that the organisation is prepared to take. Our experience is that keeping a focus on overall riskiness puts the detailed work of reviewing individual risks in context."

Summary

This chapter had two objectives. The first was to outline a practical and usable risk management process by outlining the key steps of the process and the questions that need to be answered by each step. The second was to share some of our experiences of how to facilitate the risk management process in a way that:

- Engages the right people at the right time
- Uses approaches that energise people and keep the energy throughout
- Focuses on the role of the facilitator as a risk process expert, but also as a vegetarian who stays out of the 'meat' of the situation, empowering the group to be accountable for the process outputs.

The tried and tested approaches in this chapter work for us and should provide enough guidance for you to try different approaches from which you can develop your own.

It is important to remember that an effective risk facilitator cannot make risk management work all on their own. The organisation will need governance that supports risk management and provides a decision-making regime that can make good decisions in risky and important situations.

Workshops are a part of the solution, where they are designed to achieve a specific purpose. The next chapter will go into more details of how to plan and deliver successful risk workshops.

Questions for reflection

1. Where are the areas where you have typically facilitated different parts of the risk process in one session – might you get better results taking a different approach?
2. Are there some areas where facilitating a group process would be better served by gaining individual input?
3. Where might you be able to use breaks in the process to reframe the information so that people have a chance to really reflect and use 'slow thinking' (see Chapter 3)?

Reference and further reading

De Bono, E. (2000). *Six thinking hats*. Penguin.

6 Risk workshops

Workshops are just part of the risk process, but they're a very important part, which we'll cover in this chapter.

Why are workshops so important? They are where representatives of different areas get together. In a workshop you are able to generate ideas as a group, build consensus and agreement, and come up with decisions. Often, you can sort out differences and misunderstandings immediately. If you design your process well, you can build shared ownership of outcomes. In workshops people can be listened to, feel heard by others, and give voice to concerns. When people have the opportunity to work together on outputs, workshops can be so much more than dumping grounds of all of the risks that people could dream up individually. In a workshop there's a chance to deal with different perceptions of what is risky and why. You can also challenge biases that can so easily occur, such as 'groupthink' or other sources of bias as covered in Chapter 3. All of these workshop benefits only come with good facilitation.

Workshops can work very well as part of the process. But they're *not* the whole process. Many people try to do everything as a workshop, whereas a mixture of larger workshops, small subgroups, and one-to-one work is more likely to be successful. See Chapter 5 for our recommendations on how to create the right mix.

DOI: 10.4324/9781003245858-6

84 Risk workshops

The world is shifting to make more use of virtual workshops, sometimes with all participants fully remote and at other times using a hybrid mix with some people in the room and some people participating from afar. Chapter 7 will deal with the additional challenges to overcome in these cases and should be read alongside the suggestions in this chapter, the vast majority of which still apply.

Workshops give us an opportunity to do something different and creative and to break out of what has been a formulaic way of dealing with risk in many organisations.

Here's an example of a successful half-day risk workshop that is still having an impact.

> Tony, who works in local government in Wales, recalled a risk identification workshop for the regeneration of Cardiff Harbour. It lasted half a day but is still having a positive impact years later.
>
> He talked through how they got it right. "We brought in external facilitators and had a good range of stakeholders present. We came up with a huge range of risks, from World War II unexploded bombs to alien invasion!" Tony went on to explain that alien invasion didn't mean little green men from Mars, but rather the possibility of the ecosystem in a new freshwater lake getting out of balance. This could mean plagues of midges and other small insects, which would spoil the new environment for local people and visitors, including wedding guests nearby. Tony described how they set aside funding, which allowed them to reduce this risk by stocking the lake with fish and injecting insecticide into mud to kill off midge larvae. A few years later, the risk became an issue (the risk actually occurred) and further measures were needed.

Cardiff Bay has been visited by teams from as far afield as Italy, Korea, and the USA as a case study for controlling alien invasion. Tony has continued to be committed to risk. He's found the way to keep risk alive in his authority. "With the right people, who all care about what we're doing, it'll stay on the agenda!"

That workshop certainly worked for Tony. How can you make yours as successful?

Let's look at risk workshops in three parts:

1. The work you do beforehand to prepare for a workshop
2. Running the workshop itself
3. How you can get actions completed after the workshop is over.

PREPARING FOR A WORKSHOP

Learning from experience

What's the very first thing you do when you start to think about a risk workshop? Penny suggests you start by looking back. What can you learn from previous risk workshops and how can you build on your experiences there? What went well that you should continue this time and what do you want to do differently? By doing this for every workshop, you'll be tapping into your own learning and improving as you go.

Purpose

The key question to answer for workshops is 'What is the purpose?' What is the point of running this particular workshop at this time?

Agree the purpose of your workshop with your senior manager or client and be clear on the benefits of doing this work together.

Remember that the workshop is just one part of a bigger process. It helps to explain a clear vision of what's important and why, as well as the benefits of doing this workshop. Are there any issues, conflicts, or politics that they can share which could affect this workshop? These are likely to be sources of risk too.

What are the objectives?

What do you want to have achieved by the end of your risk workshop? Detailed objectives will derive from the purpose, answering this question for the workshop: 'Today we will . . .' Usually, four or five objectives keep the detail at the right level.

Who should be there and for which parts of this workshop?

The purpose of your workshop will inform who should be there, and, just as important, who should not. Remember, too, that not everybody needs to be there for the whole time. You might want some specialists to come in just for a small part of the session. How many people should be there? It's often good to get representatives of the different areas concerned – you'll find guidelines for who should take part in a variety of types of workshops in Chapter 5. Remember, too, that workshops become less efficient with larger numbers. Think through who you need to make this part of the process work and make sure you have people from the right levels within your organisation, as well as the right number and at the right times.

What roles are needed for an effective workshop?

There are at least three roles needed, in addition to the people focusing on the risks.

1. There's the *risk facilitator*, who facilitates the meeting. As such, their role is to stay out of the details of the content. They need to be able to challenge people about their perception of risks.

2. *Timekeeper:* It helps to appoint someone else to keep an eye on how much time is left and how you're progressing through the agenda. Their role is to keep you on track.
3. A *recorder (or scribe)* can capture the output, including decisions and actions, so that they can be shared immediately afterwards.

How we work together . . .

An important element of workshops is usually left out, although its inclusion makes a big difference. This is to set *very clear ground rules*, or ways of working. We suggest talking about 'how we work together' rather than mentioning 'rules', as this is more encouraging. Preferably, when you have time and especially if conflict is likely, gather them from the group before agreeing how you'll work together. This step gives you a chance to anticipate problems and address them up front before they occur. By anticipating problems in this way, the risk facilitator has a much better chance of a successful workshop. Some examples of ground rules include:

1. How people will use mobiles and laptops; a common rule here is to keep mobiles on silent and laptops closed during the workshop sessions, but not breaks
2. Respecting confidentiality; which aspects of the workshop need to be kept secret and why; you might agree to allow all information to be shared, but keep the name of the contributor anonymous, for example
3. One tip that I find very useful is to write down 'spellling dusn't mattter'; it normally raises a laugh and takes the pressure off anybody who is writing in public, especially anyone with dyslexia.

Plan to record actions and decisions accurately during the workshop

How are you going to keep track of actions and decisions? Can the scribe write them out? If somebody is going to type them up, can you make them visible to everyone in real time? How are you going to make sure that everyone is clear on the next steps? How will you follow up to make sure actions are done after the workshop?

What about hidden agendas?

Are there likely to be any hidden agendas? Plan to find these out beforehand to uncover other aspects of politics which could affect your workshop. If you're fairly new to risk facilitation, check with somebody experienced to make sure that nothing has been missed.

What about the timing of the workshop?

How long should a workshop last? There is always a balance to strike between maintaining energy and making maximum use of the time that people can be together. There are some creative options you can use to get this balance right. Chapter 5 has much more to say on this, including some tips on how many risk workshops may be needed to cover the whole risk management process.

Choosing your activities

What will the process be for taking you from the opening of your workshop to completion, having met your objectives? In Chapter 5 we highlighted those steps where risk workshops are useful for risk management, and, for each step, the questions to be answered and the outputs to be produced. Choose activities to deliver these, as appropriate, as well as meeting your workshop goals. You'll need general activities as well, such as those to get started by welcoming and introducing participants to one another. Other activities include energisers, sharing information, gathering ideas, analysing, evaluating, problem solving, gaining agreement, making decisions, and ending workshops well. There is much more on each of these, and on workshops in general, in Penny's book *Making Workshops Work* (Pullan, 2021). Make sure that you design your workshop to be engaging and interesting with a variety of activities.

Designing for people

Remember that your participants will come with their own personalities and biases! As you plan for your workshop and design the activities, bear in mind the conscious, subconscious, and affective influences that are likely to affect the individuals in your workshop and the group as a whole. It's a good idea to review Chapter 3 again before finalising your plans and before running the workshop. What can you do to use framing and reframing to help the group break out of fixed thought patterns? What can you do to help the group to reflect and become more aware? Where can you use techniques to get independent input from individuals in the workshop context?

What preliminary work should be done?

As the facilitator you will want to prepare carefully. Do you have enough resources available, including an appropriate place to meet? For each particular workshop you can check for the inputs you'll need from previous parts of the process, as shown in Chapter 5.

How well do people coming to this workshop understand risk?

Their understanding may be very basic. Often people will require a quick reminder of the basics as laid out in Chapter 2.

What about the diversity of the group?

Do you need to plan carefully in this area? For example, if you have somebody who is known to be very loud and you have others who are likely to be very quiet, how will you handle that? What about people at differing levels of seniority within the organisation? If you have a mixture of hierarchies in the room, it's important not to ignore this as it will affect the dynamics in the room. One option is to form small, mixed groups that then feed back to the whole workshop. Another option is to use some forms of anonymous input.

What about the mixture of professionals? For example, engineers and marketing specialists often behave quite differently in workshops. What about cross-cultural issues? These can be as much between organisations as between people from different countries. There are many things that influence people's attitude to specific risks. Ensure that you have covered the different needs of every participant and design your workshop to meet their needs. Thinking how you will deal with diversity in advance will help you prepare for a great workshop.

Invite people and keep them informed

Once your purpose is clear, use it as you invite appropriate participants, so they can set aside time for the workshop. It makes sense to do this well in advance. Detailed joining information sent out before the session should contain the purpose of the meeting, the objectives, the time plan, who is participating, where to go for the workshop, and include links to any preparatory information. Ensure that all the other resources are available for the day, from the meeting room to the materials you need.

Workshop environment

Where will you hold the workshop? How can you create the right atmosphere? Think of all five senses, and how you can use them to create a good environment.

1 *Sight:* natural light keeps people much more alert than fluorescent light, so avoid dark basement rooms. Make sure that everyone can see any shared material, such as recorded risks and actions.

2 *Sound:* the best background for effective work is a quiet and peaceful room away from traffic noise and free from loud air conditioning.
3 *Touch:* are the chairs comfortable? Are the tables clean?
4 *Taste:* have you provided some food to keep people going? Fresh fruit or nuts are more effective than biscuits and cakes as they avoid a sugar high and the subsequent crash.
5 *Smell:* is the room stuffy after a previous meeting? Can you open the windows?

The environment for virtual workshops needs a different approach – see Chapter 7.

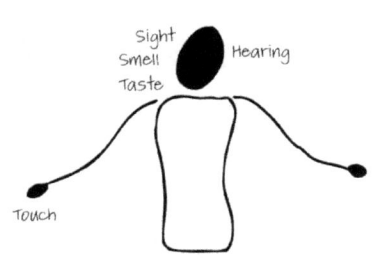

Risks and issues for your workshop

While your workshop will be about risks and issues, there are other risks and issues for you consider – the ones that relate to your workshop! What risks are there that could impact your workshop? What issues already exist that you need to deal with? It makes sense to go through a simple risk management process to identify and consider whether to respond to the risks that you face around your session.

DURING THE WORKSHOP

We recommend that you have a plan for your risk workshop, with processes and resources in place from start to finish. However, facilitated workshops seldom run to plan! You have to be prepared to divert if your initial plan doesn't work quite as well as you had hoped. If you've prepared well and have a range of options, then things are likely to run much more smoothly.

Before you begin, you might find it helpful to kick off your workshop with a senior sponsor or manager summarising why this particular workshop is important to your organisation.

92 Risk workshops

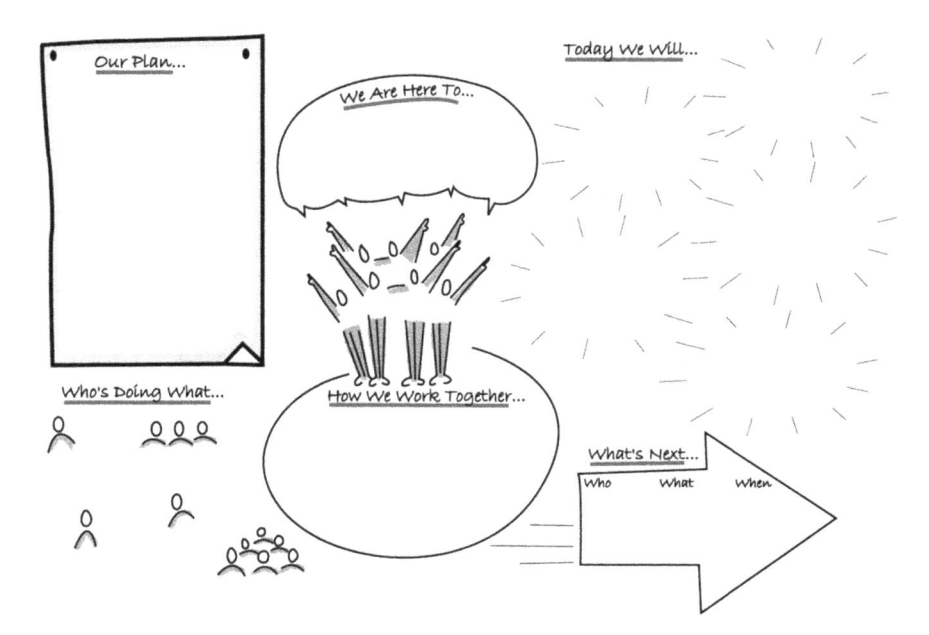

Figure 6.1 The Magic 6™ steps to start up any workshop (from Pullan, *Virtual Leadership*, 2nd edition – used with permission)

At the start of a workshop, run through all the steps shown in Figure 6.1. If you've prepared carefully and communicated carefully with everyone beforehand, this should just be a reprise for everyone. It provides the group with the opportunity to have their input and make changes if necessary.

1 *We are here to:* what's the purpose of your workshop today? Once this is agreed, display it so that everyone can see it. This will help you keep on track.
2 *Today we will:* what do you want to achieve by the end; what are the objectives for the meeting?
3 *Our plan:* what is the agenda? What happens when?
4 *Who's doing what:* what are the roles and who will play them? Choose a timekeeper and a scribe at this point of the meeting if you haven't already done so.

5 *How we work together:* what are the ground rules? This step is very important to anticipate problems and to make it clear how the workshop will run.
6 *What's next:* talk about how actions will be captured and followed up.

Introduce risk management

Run through the key risk concepts needed for this particular workshop at the start, so that everyone is clear.

How do you keep to time?

The facilitator needs to strike a balance between the needs of some to go into detail and the time available. For example, in a workshop that is planning responses to previously identified and prioritised risks, you may need to intervene to stop too much discussion about lower priority risks. Our experience is that people can get carried away discussing risks they care much about, but which in the greater scheme of things don't warrant the airtime. These could be low probability/low impact risks, for example. The facilitator has a crucial role here to move the group along, while at the same time acknowledging the importance of the risk to the people involved. Here's an example:

> "We've spent the last hour discussing risks in the Human Resources area. We have five other areas to cover today. Should we continue in HR and schedule a further workshop for tomorrow for the other areas, or should we move on now? What's your view?"

Keeping people engaged and interested

With a variety of activities lined up and a welcoming and interesting environment, your risk workshop is off to a good start. But how can you keep people engaged? Here are some ideas:

- Vary what you (and they) do
- Use visual representations rather than just words (for example, plot risks on graphs rather than just writing long lists or viewing spreadsheets)
- Use stories to hook people in and engage them to the end of the story
- Use the brain: get people curious and bring in new and unexpected things
- Get people out of their seats.

Key to much of this is keeping each participant's brain and body in an appropriate state for each activity. By changing the focus on their brain and/or what their body is doing, their state will change.

How do you stay calm as facilitator?

Although it's critical for the process to have energy, the facilitator needs to find a way of remaining calm throughout. The very nature of workshops is that you cannot predict what will happen. To prevent unexpected situations getting to you, it's useful to have tactics for staying calm, using both your brain's focus and what your body is doing.

At the start, you might find it helpful to 'anchor' your mind to a successful workshop in the past. Remember that you don't always have to be busy doing or saying something. Often quiet thought, rather than a quick response, will stand you in good stead. You really need to be able to manage your own state as a facilitator, staying centred and effective, even when things get tough.

One helpful way of doing this is to reflect back what you see happening in the group, rather than taking it upon yourself to 'fix' the group.

Remember that the group owns the risks, and the group owns the results. The facilitator doesn't. The group can decide what to do as a result. It takes the pressure off the risk facilitator. This technique has been important for Penny as she moved from working with small project groups to large international programmes of change.

What do you do during the workshop if it all goes horribly wrong?

Risk facilitators are often anxious about things going wrong in their sessions and wonder what they would do. Of course, things often don't go as planned. One obvious tactic if things take a turn for the worse is to take a short break. This is often quite as much of a relief to the group, as to the facilitator. Often, a simple chat with people individually will put the workshop back on track. Try not to be 'in control and in charge' but facilitate the group to do their best. The biggest mistake you can make is to behave as if it's your workshop and you own the outputs. This isn't true, as it is the group's workshop, and they own the outputs. It would be far better to acknowledge the issues and ask the group for their suggestions. If you are concerned about failure, read through Chapter 8 and make sure you've covered the potential pitfalls of risk workshops.

How are you going to gather input?

You might want to use brainstorming. A crucial ground rule for gathering a large number of ideas in this way is to make sure that all contributions are constructive, rather than negative or critical. It's the facilitator's job to ensure this by challenging anyone who comes up with negative comments at this early stage. The group will be able to judge all the contributions once the creative part is over.

Another good way of gathering input is to encourage people to share lessons learned from previous work.

Use the fact that you will have more than one workshop. The time in between workshops is ideal for the participants to go away and come back with thought-through ideas to the next step.

Use anonymous input to good effect

You can use anonymous ways of gathering input to get the widest possible range of ideas. This works especially when you have a wide range of people with different levels of power in the organisation or when people prefer not to speak controversial ideas out loud. In an in-person meeting you can ask people to write on sticky notes and stick them up.

Another way of gathering risk ideas in person is to cover a table with paper. Give everyone a set of pens of the same colour and ask them to stand around the table. Write the question in the centre. For example, 'What are all the risks that might happen to this project?' Ask everybody to write down everything that comes to mind. Then get the group to move slowly around the table adding on further comments until they return TO where they started. This is a very quick way to gather a large number of ideas from a group. Figure 6.2

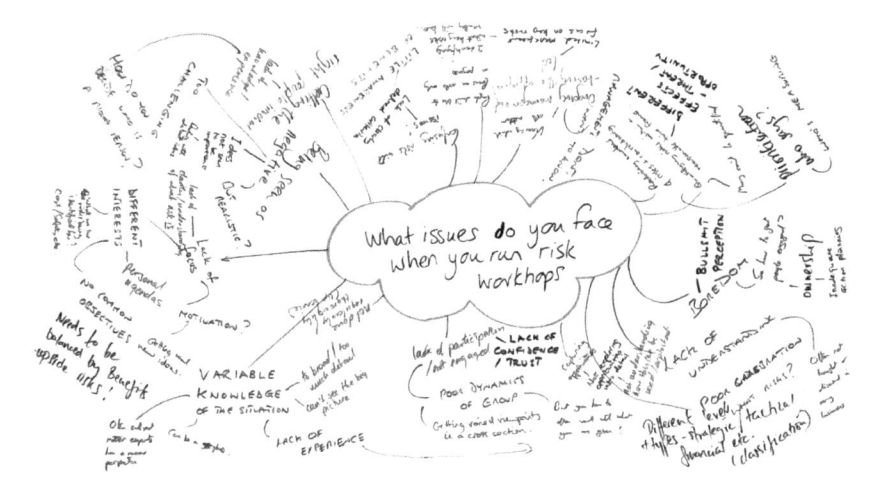

Figure 6.2 A group map built by APM members about the issues they face with risk workshops (used with permission)

is an example used to gather issues people face in risk workshops as part of the research for Chapter 8 (thanks to the Association for Project Management (APM) Programme Management Specific Interest Group).

> Penny used the group mind-map technique where she only had 20 minutes for a workshop on a major programme. When she joined the programme, it had a mantra: 'We have a thousand ways to fail, but we proceed valiantly'. The first thing Penny did was to spend all 20 minutes running a risk identification workshop. You should have seen the relief on the faces of the people involved, as they realised that the risky areas had actually been identified and were going to be investigated. They wouldn't have to wake up in the middle of the night in cold sweats as they thought of yet more unidentified risks ever again!

Visible information

It can be very helpful and engaging for groups to see what they've been talking about. So how can you make the discussion visible to people? Penny uses techniques of recording words and pictures to make sure that all the ideas are visible to the whole group. An example of this might be each person writing down their own ideas on sticky notes and then presenting them in clusters on a wall. Alternatively, the risk facilitator or scribe can write down risks on a flipchart, board, or shared screen as they are raised.

Participants are people!

Your participants are individual human beings, each with their own personalities and biases, which we covered in Chapter 3. Do you remember the three key ways to help groups make more informed and rational decisions under uncertainty? These will be useful to practise during your session and there is more on how in Chapter 3.

Team stages

It's good practice to make sure you are aware how teams form: the common stages that all teams go through. One way of understanding this is by using the Tuckman Team Development Model. This predicts four stages in turn:

1. *Forming:* where the team come together
2. *Storming:* where people jostle for position
3. *Norming:* where people begin to settle down into group 'norms'
4. *Performing:* where the team work together effectively.

Knowing that these stages are going to happen, it makes sense to include introductions to help the team form and ground rules to help the team to 'norm'. Facilitators who know that 'storming' typically comes before 'norming' will expect some disagreements and want to resolve these to move on. For the team to really 'perform', the facilitator must help to create a productive atmosphere where people bring their energy to the task in hand.

It's helpful to be aware of a range of models because different models have elements which work better in different situations and which highlight different aspects of team working. No model is completely right on its own in all situations. Another that we've used to good effect is the Drexler/Sibbet Team Performance Model (Sibbet, 2011). We particularly like this model as it makes it very clear that team performance depends on establishing good foundations for team working at the start of the workshop. It shows clearly how the team need to be clear on their purpose and to build trust before clarifying goals and gaining commitment. Only then does action follow, and possibly high performance. The model uses the analogy of a bouncing ball: the more effort put in upfront, the higher the ball will bounce.

Conflict

Be aware of conflict. In fact, you should expect it. Conflict just means that there are some disagreements, with a sprinkling of tension. There are different perspectives on the work you're doing. Use them, don't hide them. You get better decisions when there has been some element of this 'task conflict'. Another form of conflict is 'process conflict', where people disagree on the way you're going about things.

If conflict appears, you'll need to sort it out immediately. To do so, highlight what you see happening, rather than 'sweeping it under the carpet' and hoping it will go away. It won't. Refer people back to the ground rules that you agreed at the start of the session and ask them to abide by these. You may need to come up with some new ones as a group to deal with any issues. Consider calling a break and talking with the individuals concerned. Remember to stay neutral and to focus on what you can see and hear, rather than judgements and inferences. Another useful to tip is to 'be hard on the issue, yet soft on the person'. Keep the group focused on the work issue at hand and not on personalities.

You don't want to have personal relationship conflict, or even fights, breaking out within your risk workshop. If you know that such relationship conflict is likely to arise, you'll need to prepare even more thoroughly than usual, carefully discussing issues with the people concerned and keeping those people separate as far as possible. Do they even need to be there together?

Make sure that actions and decisions are clearly agreed and documented

Do this during the session and then circulate them as quickly as possible afterwards. What is going to be done by whom and by when? The right place to document the outputs is almost always the risk register. Unfortunately, this is all too often a dead document, gathering dust, rather than the central repository for all risk-based decisions. There is no need for detailed minutes, as these are likely to remain unread. Agree how the actions will be followed up and how will they be reported back to the group.

Will people do their actions?

Ask people about their intentionality – this is the strength of their intent to carry out each action. Penny uses a scale of one to ten and asks people at the end of workshops to report how likely they are to get each action done. If they're unsure that they will be able to do the actions, then she adjusts the action. Surely it is far better to have an imperfect action that's completed, than a perfect one that isn't?

Lessons learned

While many organisations talk about 'lessons learned', too often these become lessons filed away or even lessons forgotten. What a waste! The risk facilitator can ensure that their risk workshops improve over time by identifying lessons learned with their groups during risk workshops *and* then agreeing actions to take in future workshops as a result. This can be done as simply as taking 5 minutes to explore 'what went well' and 'I wish that . . .' (Framing things positively is a much more powerful way to learn than 'what went wrong'.)

AFTER THE WORKSHOP

It's very important to share actions and decisions as quickly as possible. Penny likes to take photographs of outputs from in-person meetings and share them immediately, rather than have the details typed up, as these provide a strong visual reminder on top of the formal risk register and it is so much quicker.

Follow up of actions

Without follow up, actions tend not to happen. Follow up is ideally discussed and agreed at the end of the workshop before everyone leaves. Ideally, your actions can be added to your project, programme or operations plan immediately after your workshop, as well as to your risk register, so they'll be tracked as part of day-to-day work.

How will you keep risk management alive for the rest of the process?

Ensure that you have identified owners of different risk areas. How will you engage these people going forward? Too many risk identification workshops end up with a completed risk register that is subsequently forgotten about. While this may tick boxes for audit or compliance, it is of no practical use. As the risk facilitator, it's your job to bring energy and life into the process.

You'll need to feed information back to the appropriate people, perhaps managers in your organisation, your project sponsor and/or the board, or your client. How will you do this?

Summary

Risk workshops are an inevitable part of the risk management process. It's essential to prepare in advance to ensure you have the best chance of a successful workshop. Facilitating workshops well is an art and experiencing good risk facilitation is very different from reading it in a book. You will find more helpful hints and tools when you sign up for them at this book's website at www.makingriskwork.com, as well as ongoing updates on our work.

In the next chapter, we explore running virtual risk workshops where participants can't all get together in person. We give you additional hints and tips to help you as you prepare, run, and make actions happen through fully remote or hybrid participants.

Questions for reflection

1 Looking back, what has worked well in your risk workshops in the past? What do you wish you could do differently next time?
2 What changes will you make to planning and running your next workshop?
3 What might you do differently to keep people engaged beyond workshops?
4 How will your insights about human perception from Chapter 3 change how you run your risk workshops going forward?

References and further reading

Pullan, P. (2021). *Making workshops work: Creative collaboration for our time*. Practical Inspiration Publishing.

Sibbet, D. (2011). *Visual Teams: Graphic tools for commitment, innovation, & high performance*. Wiley, 36–37.

Tuckmann, B. R. (1965). Developmental sequence in small groups. *Psychological Bulletin, 63*, 384–399.

7 Making virtual risk management work, whether fully remote or hybrid

In this chapter, we explore the situations where people can't all get together in person to manage risk. Instead, they work from different locations, the main office, home, co-working spaces, or remote offices. Sometimes everyone works remotely. This new virtual world means that those of us who facilitate risk need to adapt and make risk work in this situation.

In this chapter we'll explore tips and practical strategies for making risk work across distance throughout the risk management process. While risk workshops obviously provide new challenges when people are dispersed, we'll cover other aspects beyond workshops, too.

Context

Penny first went virtual when her flight to New York on 13 September 2001 was cancelled by the 9/11 tragedy stopping commercial flights. She had been due to travel to host a kick-off meeting for a global programme and was looking forward to meeting everyone. They would have spent a couple of weeks together, sorting everything out and setting up the risk processes for the programme. Instead, a terrorist attack changed everything. She had to get things done with colleagues around the world without being able to meet in person. Instead, they relied on 2001 technology to get together – audio conference calls while sharing screens online and video calls from the special video suite, not their own laptops! Included in this work was the entire risk management process. Since then, Penny

DOI: 10.4324/9781003245858-7

has carried out risk management in virtual settings, both fully remote and hybrid, for the last 20 years, and the use of virtual work has grown slowly over this time.

In 2020, huge numbers of people around the world had a similar experience as COVID-19 lockdowns meant people had to work from home if they could. There was an overnight transition to fully remote, virtual working and, despite this huge change, people were able to get things done. Now virtual working is proven to be a valid option for almost all organisations. Not everyone wants to be remote all the time though. Many employees enjoy a hybrid form of working, visiting the office a day or two a week and working from home the rest of the time. Risk facilitators now need to be able to make risk work in this environment, not just when everyone is always present in person in the same space.

Several words have appeared already describing the nature of this work, and it's important to get clear on precisely what they mean in this book. Taking each in turn:

- Virtual: geographically dispersed, with people working together despite the fact that at least one person is not in the same location as the others
- Remote: *everyone* is in a different physical location from the rest of the group
- Hybrid: *some* people are working together in person in the same physical location alongside *others*, who are working in different physical locations.

(Note that for individual workers there is a second meaning of hybrid which applies to their own individual working patterns. To work in a hybrid way means a mixture of some days working from home or another space, such as a co-working hub, and other days where they commute to the office and work there. We won't discuss this type of hybrid working further. Going forward, when we mention hybrid, we are referring to some people in one location with others joining from different places, as in the definition above.)

What has changed and what hasn't

Most of what we have covered so far in this book doesn't change with the shift to virtual. The fundamentals and processes of risk management apply. People and their perceptions matter just as much, and some biases become even more important: remember the conscious factor of proximity introduced in Chapter 3? This can relate to situations when a possibility of a risk materialising is either close by (we think it's more likely to occur) or far away (less likely to occur), but it also has an effect when people are either nearby (in the same room) or far away (joining remotely). The proverb 'out of sight, out of mind' is very pertinent. This proximity factor obviously plays a huge part when some people are remote from others, as their inputs are likely to be de-prioritised. Risk facilitation and the role of the risk facilitator become even more important to be able to ensure that all voices are heard and all perspectives taken into account.

The most obvious impact of going virtual on risk processes is on risk workshops. Here the choice of format plays an important part: choose the right technology platforms to suit the nature of the workshop and the format, whether fully remote or hybrid, to support the work that people will do together. Plans, processes, and how facilitators run workshops all need to adapt to cope with the challenge of engaging remote participants in risk work, especially when the work required is detailed and, unless designed otherwise, is likely to be long-winded and tedious.

The additional challenge of hybrid workshops is that they are asymmetric. There is no level playing field between those in a room together, who can easily pick up on the nuances, dynamics, and subtleties of conversation with each other or over coffee in a break, and those who are remote, limited to on-screen interaction. A key challenge is how to level this playing field.

Virtual leadership

An important concept here is virtual leadership. To work effectively with risk management in these new environments, we need to step into virtual leadership. It's far more than just being able to use the appropriate communication technology. It's about being able to engage people to identify, own, and manage risk wherever they are.

What does this mean? Figure 7.1 shows the layers of development of a competent virtual leader, whether operating with a fully remote group or in hybrid mode. Not everyone will need each of the outermost aspects, but the core is the foundation. We'll explore this model, starting in the centre and moving outwards.

To become a virtual leader, start with *self*. Explore your own mindset about what leadership means in a world where people are dispersed. Perhaps you are used to command-and-control leadership, whereas what works best virtually is a much more facilitative style, making it easy for everyone to contribute their best work wherever they are. This aligns well with what we've described throughout the rest of the book. Listening is always important when working with people but making an effort to do this well becomes even more important when some are remote and hard to hear. Personal organisation is key – preparation and thinking everything through before virtual meetings will make a positive difference and things will run much more smoothly. Patience is a virtue when working virtually, as technology can and does go wrong. The ability to keep going despite problems and to be transparent about these, while remaining confident and positive, will all help.

Working with *others* virtually brings in many important aspects. Knowing each person you work with will really help; it's helpful to know, at least to some extent, their personality, their preferences,

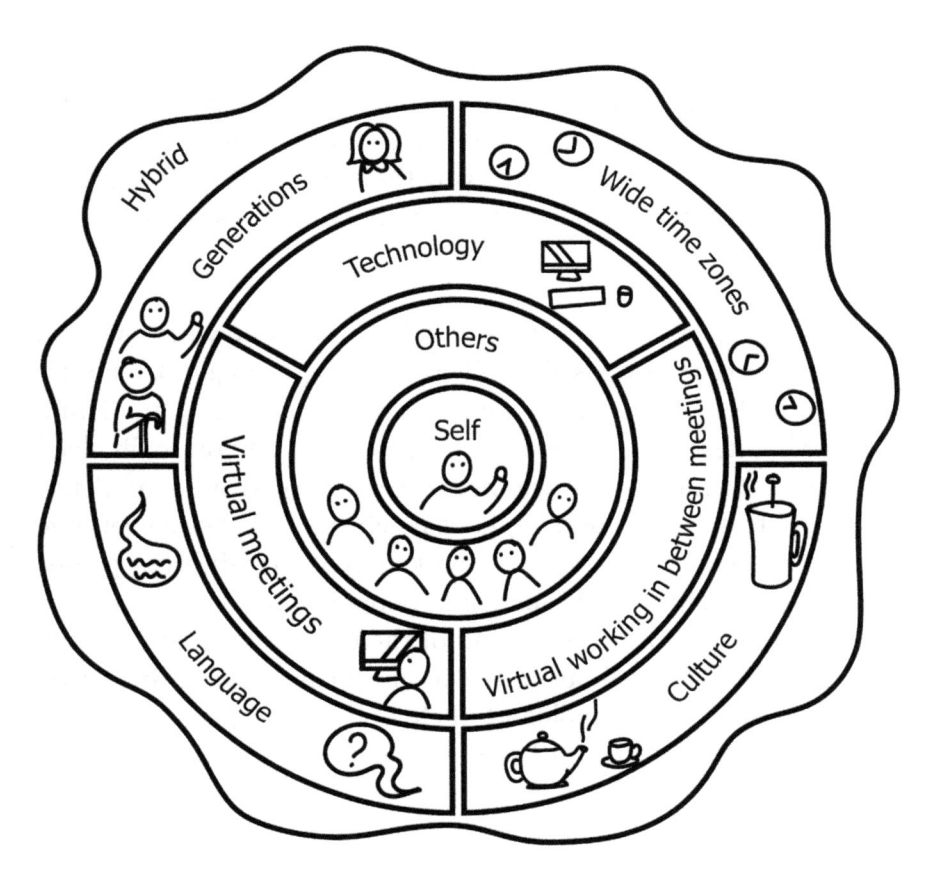

Figure 7.1 Virtual Leadership Model, from *Virtual Leadership* (Pullan, 2022; used with permission)

their skills, their motivations, and their working environment, including their access to and competence with technology. It's important to build common ground to connect with each other, and your knowledge about people helps here. Trust is foundational to virtual teams, so work on building that as people experience you, each other, and the organisation. Be fair and equitable with different people across your group. What structures make sense for the risk management work you will be doing together? As virtual teams increase in size, the number of relationships required to be maintained goes up exponentially, along with the complexity, so choose smaller team sizes that are appropriate to work you will do together. For work over time, consider how to take your ongoing virtual team to high performance: a clue, it's not just about setting goals but also that everyone knows each other, why they are there, and what they bring to the team, and knows that there is a sense of a shared vision and purpose.

Technology is obviously the foundation, without which virtual working becomes impossible. There is a huge range of technology available, so don't just use the ubiquitous video call. Think about what needs to be done and when – whether you really need to gather for a meeting or whether you can work together at different times to suit each person, i.e. asynchronously. Does everyone need to be present for all of the workshop or can different people join different parts? Perhaps some people would be fine with a recording or even a transcription of the discussion that they can peruse later? Think about how you can bring risks to life, even remotely, by using technology to help you engage people through visual means or stories rather than just sharing endless spreadsheet cells.

It's important to remember that technology is foundational, but it is not everything. Too many risk facilitators leading virtual sessions focus too much on the technology to the detriment of other aspects of virtual leadership. It's rather like electricity in a house in the UK. While it would be very difficult to live in the UK in the twenty-first century without electricity, once it is in place, they focus on making a house a home without thinking too much about their electricity supply. For me, while I couldn't write this chapter and get it to my co-author without power to run my laptop, I forget about power until I'm out and about with an empty battery! Once it works and you have the right tech for the task in hand, let's focus more on those things which make work run smoothly, helping groups be able to work together effectively.

Table 7.1 What works when – virtual tools for synchronous and asynchronous work

Synchronous tools (same time)	Tools which can be used as both synchronous and asynchronous	Asynchronous tools (accessed at different times)
Audio-only calls (such as phone calls)	Direct messaging	Voice messages
Video meetings (with the potential for shared screens)	Shared virtual whiteboards	Recordings of meetings; transcriptions of recordings of meetings
	Collaboration tools	Physical post – especially useful if sending thank you letters
		Discussion boards, collaboration tools
		Social media

We will discuss risk workshops (*virtual meetings*) and asynchronous risk management work (*virtual working in between meetings*) in the rest of this chapter, along with the complications of virtual through *wide time zones* and working through differences in *culture, language,* and *generations*. The whole framework is helpful for risk management work with *hybrid* groups, and we'll touch on the particular challenges that hybrid brings as we go through.

Virtual risk workshops

Much stays the same when risk workshops go virtual. The key steps: planning and running the workshop, as well as ensuring actions are followed up, remain the same as in Chapter 6. There are *additional* things to consider when designing virtual workshops, particularly around timing and engagement, as well as those aspects that differ between fully remote and hybrid, such as making the most of technology and ensuring the environment will work for everyone.

PLANNING

A major difference for all virtual sessions is that they need to be shorter. Groups run out of steam more quickly online, so I suggest each session is no longer than 90 minutes, and preferably an hour. With proper breaks between sessions, it may be possible to run a workshop with several sessions in one day. Think carefully, though, about how important it is for your participants to be alert and not tired. You may find it much better to run several sessions over a period of days rather than cramming a workshop into one day. Indeed, the risk management process works much better broken down into multiple workshops, so in many ways, this is ideal. With breaks, it is important to get people to leave their screens, look into the distance, and to move around. Penny encourages people to go outside if they can and gives a 30-minute break mid-morning for a half-day workshop, in addition to shorter coffee breaks when required. Another difference is that virtual sessions work best with limited numbers. I'd suggest a maximum of 10–12 in a virtual workshop, with much work done in smaller breakout groups of 3–5 people.

A key challenge of virtual risk workshops, whether fully remote or hybrid, is to keep all participants engaged and doing great work together, even when the work required is detailed and potentially, unless designed otherwise, long-winded and heavy-going. You'll find suggestions on how to engage people in Chapter 6, which we expand here. Keep activities varied so that there are no long stretches of the same thing done over and over again. (We've seen this too often when people work through long lists of risks in a very monotonous way. Instead, make it easy for them to stay interested, curious, and engaged.) While people need to watch the screen to interact, build in times for thinking when they can think and move away from the screen for a while. Get people working in small groups, via breakout rooms, and then they can feed back to everyone. In a hybrid setting, those participants who are physically together can form small groups in person in parallel with online breakout groups. Visuals are really powerful for virtual sessions as they engage the brain and communicate a holistic picture much more quickly than a string of written or spoken words. People are likely to be distracted by other things around them, so anything that will draw them in is helpful – stories are particularly useful here as they hook people in and, once hooked, they'll stay right to the end. Aim for creative collaboration, to keep people interested and engaged throughout.

When planning activities, ensure that they can be adapted for virtual use and consider how to make them creative and engaging.

Don't forget to consider risks and issues around your own risk workshop, whether hybrid or fully remote. In addition to the advice in the last chapter, the virtual nature of the workshop will bring up quite a few, which you will need to handle. For example, we have noticed how people often join virtual meetings late, and you can't just go and physically find them! That's a known issue. There is always the risk of broadband failure – it happened to Penny recently when, horror of horrors, her home broadband cut out for a day, but she had a backup in place, as she had followed the process.

Now we'll consider particular aspects to consider when planning different types of virtual workshops, first fully remote and then hybrid.

Considerations when planning fully remote workshops

The advantage of everyone being remote is that, as long as technology and internet access are good enough for every participant, there is equality between people. Each person has their own small space on a shared screen. In many ways, this equality makes fully remote workshops easier to facilitate than hybrid sessions.

It can be very useful to have a one-to-one call with each participant, especially before any high stakes virtual meeting, to prepare the way, check the technology works, and to hear their perspective. At this point, you can gain an insight into their level of understanding of risk management and, if needed, give them some explanation of what you'll be doing together and why. Connection and technology issues may well come to light at this stage. Excellent audio quality is particularly important so that people can hear each other speaking clearly, even more so than video quality. Video, even if not perfect, adds a richness to the communication. If people hate seeing themselves during workshops, rather than stopping their video for others, they can hide the 'self-view'.

As virtual workshop equality depends on technology and internet access, it is of paramount importance that each participant has both the equipment and access that will work for them. If you are not planning to meet each person beforehand, it can help to specify the minimum level of connection and technology (and competence with it) that will be required, especially if working across different organisations. This is especially important if you are going to use more specialised tools such as specialist collaboration tools providing virtual sticky notes, polling, annotations, and more. If you have access to these, and your participants are going to be able to make the most of them, we recommend these over just sharing spreadsheet cells, especially if the participants are familiar with them already. They allow a very interactive and visual experience of working with risk.

You have no control over the environment around each remote participant, but you could ask them to join from a space that will work well, letting them know what they'll need. You can't hand out materials on the day, but you can send out goody bags and perhaps materials that they will be able to use to take part: perhaps sticky notes and pens for identifying risk, along with a grid or template to use to sort them or whatever is appropriate for your needs. These help to provide variety beyond just the sense of sight and hearing. Make sure you leave enough time to guarantee they will arrive before your workshop.

Considerations when planning hybrid workshops

Instead of being easier than fully remote sessions, as many people assume before they have to run one, hybrid workshops present a major, new challenge: the lack of a level playing field. This asymmetry comes from the difference between those in a room together, who can easily pick up on the nuances and dynamics of conversation with each other, and those who are remote, limited to on-screen interaction. So, a focus with hybrid workshops must be on how to keep the playing field as level as it can be.

There are at least three types of hybrid risk workshops, and they need different considerations when planning your workshop:

1 Some participants in a physical meeting room, with others joining individually via technology from remote locations
2 Participants in a number of physical meeting rooms in different locations, connected via technology
3 A combination of the two – the most challenging of all! This combines a number of meeting rooms plus remote individuals, all connecting virtually.

Taking each option in turn:

a) Here the focus is the meeting room, so keep including the remote participants by asking them questions before those in the room. When you break into small groups, those in the room can work together, with the remote individuals joining online breakout rooms.

114 *Making virtual risk management work*

b) Here, it makes sense (where possible) to do most of the work in person in each meeting room, with everyone joining up virtually for short periods of time where necessary.
c) This is the most complex! Keep levelling the playing field for both those in secondary rooms and remote individuals.

a) One physical room, plus virtual individuals

b) Many physical rooms, connected virtually

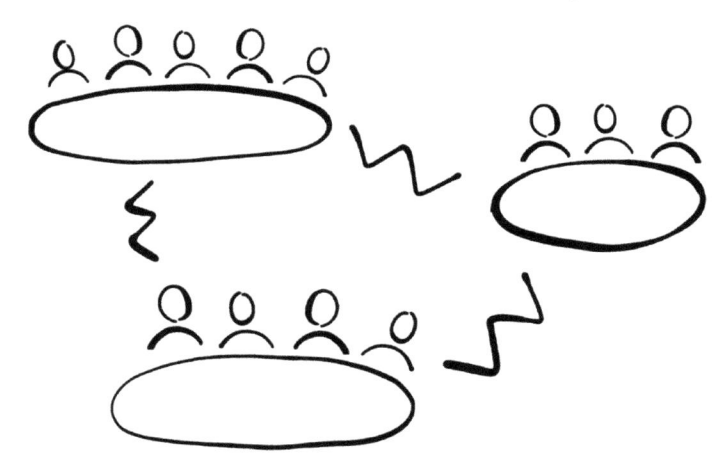

c) A combination of a & b

Figure 7.2 Types of hybrid risk workshops, from *Making Workshops Work* (Pullan, 2021; used with permission)

Just as in a fully remote set up, it makes sense to check technology (access and competence with) and the connection, but this time with any remote individuals in options a) and c) and remote rooms in b) and c). Plan to have an 'in-room' buddy to represent the remote people and who they can reach out to at any time for clarification or to share an issue. Plan for physical reminders to be displayed in the main room for all those who are remote – a name tent will do, but a life-sized cartoon cutout propped up on a chair is even better!

Just as in the fully remote case, consider sending out goody bags and tools that you'll use during the workshop to the other remote rooms and to each individual remote participant.

RUNNING

With all your planning complete, it's time to run the workshop. Be there early, making sure you have everything you need. Penny always sends out a final reminder/invitation to all participants shortly before the meeting, making it easy for them to connect when the time comes. Check the technology and connect early in case people arrive before the start time – some will.

When you start, use the Magic 6™ start-up steps from Figure 6.1. This step provides clarity that is crucial virtually, making sure everyone is clear on and agrees with the purpose, the objectives, the time plan, the roles, and the ground rules ('how we work together'). These might include additional rules for virtual such as:

- Mute if in a noisy environment
- The risk facilitator may mute others if required
- One conversation at a time
- Expect to be asked for your input every 10–20 minutes in random order; this regular polling, if agreed upfront, has the effect of people staying attentive, involved, and alert
- State your name when agreeing to an action (in a large group, for clarity).

Be aware that you won't pick up as much from participants in a virtual workshop as in person, so pay particular attention to signs of bias, as described in Chapter 3, or of the emergence of conflict, see Chapter 6, as these will need dealing with and are harder to spot. Indeed, emotions are easy to hide when remote – this can be both helpful and unhelpful. When they are obvious, some remote people find it difficult if you ask why: 'you appear angry Ruth, can you help us understand why?'

Remember to be flexible as things change, with some options up your sleeve. In hybrid workshops, do everything you can to level the playing field using the tips shared in the planning section.

Keep an eye on the energy state of individuals as sitting in front of a screen can lead to energy levels flagging more quickly. If this happens, call a short break and encourage people to get up and move around. In hybrid workshops, there is an additional need to keep focused on levelling the playing field between those in the room(s) and those remote.

It is even more likely when virtual that people will just 'go with the flow', maybe choosing to 'follow the leader', or (perhaps worse) not speak up and then not commit to the output of the session, even choosing to undermine it later. Commitment to the actions agreed in any risk session is vital. It can be tricky to check out whether there is genuine commitment to action and not just lip service when people are remote, so this needs careful planning and validation.

Virtual risk management outside of workshops

Remember that not all the risk management process is best run through workshops. Indeed, in Chapter 5 we describe how several steps can be carried out through one-to-one meetings or calls, or even asynchronously, with people working on their own and then sharing their work with yourself or the group. These all work well virtually, with one-to-one meetings via phone or video call rather than in person.

It's important to check in with remote people so that they maintain motivation and are completely clear on the work they need to do. As a risk facilitator, you probably don't have line management authority over those who are doing the work, so you'll need to facilitate, motivate, and influence people to move things along by keeping in touch, listening to what they have to say, and encouraging them.

What makes virtual more complicated . . .

From the Virtual Leadership Model in Figure 7.1, at fourth step from the centre, you can see a few aspects that make virtual just a bit more complicated: wide time zones, cultural differences, language differences, and generational differences. Let's cover each in turn:

> **Wide time zones** make working together at the same time more of a challenge, so it is logical to move to fewer live meetings and more asynchronous working. In this case, most of the risk management work should be done outside of workshops and then, where necessary, people come together for short meetings, preferably when office hours overlap. If there is no time slot that allows this, then it is good to 'share the pain' across the group by taking it in turns to meet outside of office hours.
> **Cultural differences** can be across national cultures, professional cultures, or even organisational cultures! While people within each culture can vary widely, the midpoint of acceptable behaviour for a group of actuaries (for example) will be somewhat different from that of a group of salespeople. Cultural differences are often understood using scales covering

areas such as this one adapted from Erin Mayer's ranges for national cultures in her book *The Culture Map (2014)*:

- How people give feedback to others
- How egalitarian or top-down leadership is
- If decisions are made by consensus or by the leader
- Whether disagreements are confronted or avoided
- How flexible time is
- Whether people communicate with lots of information about their whole lives or stick to the work topic at hand
- Whether trust is based on tasks or relationships
- Whether people persuade with principles or application first.

You can see how culture is a complex topic! When working with a culture different to your own, listen very carefully and notice what is different. Virtual working means it's even harder to notice and work out the differences. It pays to have a buddy from that culture who can help you to make sense of it and to communicate appropriately with people from that culture. One particularly challenging cross-cultural difference for Penny and Ruth with their British roots is the whole concept of saving face, which means that preserving group harmony is more important than stating what you believe to be correct, especially in front of others! When dealing with countries where this is the norm, such as India, China, and much of the Middle East, we need to ask open questions and help people to save face. Closed questions might give us the answer that the participants think we want, instead of what we need. This is very unhelpful in risk workshops where the whole point is to draw out different perceptions. A one-to-one conversation is more likely to give us good information than a large video call.

Language differences are everywhere, even between people who have English as a mother tongue! It's a good idea to slow down and to use business English when working virtually with those for whom English is not their first language. Make it acceptable to ask questions if things are not clear or difficult to understand. Listen out for problems. Ensure that the audio quality is as good as it can be.

Generational differences abound in the workplace with four generations: Baby Boomers, Generation X, Millennials, and the youngest – Generation Z. As human beings, the years when we grow up have a huge influence on how we approach the world. Generation X (like Penny), born from the mid 1960s to 1980, grew up playing cassette tapes when the Sony Walkman was exciting and new. The phone and physical letters were the only ways to connect virtually. Ruth, at the tail end of the Baby Boomers, grew up with vinyl records. Generation Z, born from the mid 1990s into the 2000s, are 'digital natives' and have always known virtual technology, such as text messaging and video calls. Our different experiences impact how we approach virtual workshops and virtual ways of working. Ruth and Penny love to chat on the phone, perhaps because as teenagers that was the only way we could talk with our friends? Our Gen Z children, though, see phones as far too formal and much prefer to send a message. Find out what your risk participants' preferences are. While these won't necessarily fit stereotypes of their generation, they are likely to be different from your own. Understanding these will help you to work virtually effectively across generations.

Summary

Virtual technology provides options for risk workshops and individual working when people can't be together in person, but making risk management work at a distance requires more than technology. It needs virtual leadership. This chapter has covered what this means, along with practical ideas for virtual risk workshops, both fully remote and hybrid, and aspects of virtual work beyond these. We've also explored areas which can make virtual work particularly challenging.

In the next chapter, we will run through a range of potential pitfalls for your risk management work, giving you hints and tips to help you avoid them.

Questions for reflection

1 How do you use virtual working for risk management – risk workshops and/or individual work?
2 Think about a virtual risk workshop you've been part of. What worked well? What would you do differently: from planning to running your next risk workshop?
3 How do you use virtual working for risk management beyond workshops now, and how do you plan to develop this further?
4 Which of the complications mentioned do you encounter now? What learning can you apply?

References and further reading

Meyer, E. (2014). *The culture map*. PublicAffairs.
Pullan, P. (2021). *Making workshops work: Creative collaboration for our time*. Practical Inspiration.
Pullan, P. (2022). *Virtual leadership: Practical strategies for success with remote or hybrid work and teams*. Kogan Page.

8 Potential pitfalls and how to overcome them

This chapter deals with the practical problems and challenges that people face when making risk management work: pitfalls that the reader of this book will be able to prepare for and avoid.

Every pitfall described in this chapter has come from a real, current risk practitioner – someone who has shared with us their concerns and frustrations about making risk management work. Some of the pitfalls are at the heart of risk management, such as people confusing risks with issues. Others are more subtle. We include them all because this chapter is designed to provide immediate help to people who are facilitating risk management.

The chapter is structured into three broad categories:

1 Pitfalls when applying the risk management process
2 Pitfalls when facilitating
3 Pitfalls when trying to create a culture where risk management works well.

Each pitfall is stated in bold italics, followed by our response on how best to tackle it. Often, there is more detail elsewhere in the book, but this chapter is meant to give quick, practical advice that the risk facilitator can apply immediately. We suggest that, rather

DOI: 10.4324/9781003245858-8

than reading this chapter in detail, you flick through the pitfalls listed below to find those of most relevance to you.

Pitfalls when applying the risk management process

In this section you'll find a range of pitfalls related to the process of risk management, along with tips to help you avoid them in the future. We covered the general principles of risk management, along with the outline of a generic process, in Chapter 2 and Chapter 5. Some of the guidance will refer you back to those earlier chapters.

We have no risk process

Chapter 5 gives you the steps in a process and hopefully you can now tailor that to suit your needs. It will be important to agree with the management team how the process will be governed and the roles people will play. Getting as much buy-in to the risk process at the start is vital.

People think that if we've got a risk register – however partial – we are doing risk management

It's important to have a risk register, so you have a start, even if your register has metaphorical cobwebs or is incomplete. The key thing is to improve the content of the risk register and the value that it brings. You could rejuvenate the risk register in a number of ways, beginning with making sure information from all the steps in the risk management process are included. For example, you could validate the risks on the register with risk owners, refreshing or deleting them as necessary.

Alternatively, you could begin the process anew and tidy the existing risk register as part of a wider risk identification exercise. You can find other ideas in Chapter 5. The key thing is to facilitate some change so that people can start to see the benefits quickly.

The people I work with don't understand the process

As a risk facilitator, one of your most important roles is to make sure that everyone has a clear understanding about the steps in the risk process and the chance to ask questions if they want to. Often people are confused about what risk management involves, and it is important to make sure that questions and misunderstandings are cleared up. Often people will understand the risk management process much better if you explain clearly which part you are focusing on at a particular time. There are different questions to be answered at each step and different skills involved in doing each step well as outlined in Chapter 5.

My manager seems to think that a complex process will fix our current problems

It won't. 'Garbage in, garbage out' applies just as much to risk management as to computer systems! The process itself is simple in principle – there's no need to make it more complicated. The difficult part of risk management is engaging the people. That is why facilitation is increasingly recognised as being so crucial.

People don't understand what risk is, or have unclear or even conflicting definitions of risk

Risks are uncertainties that matter. If something is a fact, it's not uncertain, so it can't be a risk – although it may be the cause of one or more risks. If something is uncertain, but doesn't directly affect the objectives, then it's not a risk to that work – it doesn't matter. It's a good idea to run people through the key concepts around risk before running a risk workshop or starting the risk management process.

People confuse issues with risks

Issues are known situations that need to be managed. They are not uncertain future events. Issues need to be dealt with, but not by the risk process. Although some people argue that they can effectively manage a process that deals with issue resolution and risk management together, our experience is that this does not work well for either issues or risks. There are links, of course. Issues can be causes of risks, and unmanaged risks can become issues. We strongly advise you to keep separate logs and have separate discussions of issues and risks in meetings. Otherwise risks (things that might happen) will always take second priority to issues (things actually happening) because they're more urgent, although not necessarily more important.

When I work with people, they come up with 'risks'. Often these are not risk events, but the cause or even the effect of a risk. What can I do about this frequent muddle?

It's important to make sure that people understand what a risk event is and how it differs from the cause and the effect. If you don't, then it's almost impossible to prioritise risks and make good decisions about where to focus your time. It can also be really difficult for other people to understand the risk descriptions. Using the three-part risk description set out in Chapter 2 works really well. It helps people tease out causes from risk events and events from effects, and it brings clarity to the whole process. Challenge and question people to make sure that your risk register contains risk events, rather than the background cause or the subsequent effect. Reframe statements that people have made and ask them if this is what they really meant – they are usually grateful for the clarity.

We tend to be too woolly with risks – we're not specific enough; this makes them hard to quantify or explain

Make sure that you've been clear about the big picture and risk categories before moving into the detailed work of identifying risks. Encourage people to be as specific as possible about what might happen and why when they are identifying risks. As risk facilitator, you need to challenge people to provide more detail if required. You may need to help people articulate what the event that may occur actually is, why it may occur, and how that would affect the objectives. Try using everyday language, for example: 'What are the things you are worried about?' or 'What are the things that could go better than planned without you doing anything about them?' Then tease out the cause – 'Why might that occur?' Next, tease out the effect – 'What would happen if your worry/hope came true?' Our experience is that people become skilled at this really quickly if you can help them frame their perspective on the risk in question.

All the risks we identify are obvious – so there seems that no added value is gained by going through the process

It is a common problem for people to focus mainly on what we'd call 'business-as-usual risks', that is, those things that experience tells you will always be risky in the type of work you do. The normal variability you'd expect in your work, for example based on availability of resources, should be dealt with as part of normal business planning. Risk management is about identifying and managing the 'unusual' risks. As a facilitator, you need to keep the group focused on what's special about the situation in question.

People focus on potential threats and tend to leave out potential opportunities

Always start with opportunities. It is very difficult to move into a positive mindset after dealing with threats. If your current process ignores positive opportunities, think about how you can include them. There may not be the same number of good things that might occur as bad ones, but you'll be missing a trick if you don't try. Good things might happen!

Describing opportunities is really difficult – sometimes they end up just as responses to threats

One of the biggest mistakes people make when starting to work with positive risk is to describe opportunities as binary choices – we could do x, or not. There is no chance of occurrence associated with such a statement – the outcome is in your control: you are either going to do it, or not. The objective in risk management is to focus on *potential* opportunities. These are events that might happen anyway, without any intervention. They are important because they may warrant management effort to make them more likely or to have greater impact. Risk management best practice says that we should, at least, be ready to seize potential opportunities if they occur because they are rare. So use the format to describe risks that we outlined in Chapter 2 to frame positive risks and be aware of avoiding descriptions that are just management choices. It takes a bit of practice but works really well once you've mastered the skill.

No one takes ownership of risk

First of all, see if your senior leaders are taking overall ownership of risk management. If leaders are not 'walking the talk', then it can be really difficult to get others to follow. As a facilitator, you can help to coach senior leaders about their role. More practically, you need to make sure that owners are allocated at the risk identification stage. You can also set up follow-up mechanisms for risk owners that make best use of their time. Chapter 4 has some ideas about how to do this. It's really important not to take on the risk ownership role yourself. Stay vegetarian (as described in Chapter 4). You can still offer positive support to the risk owners without inappropriately taking on their role yourself. Note: the exception to this is if you are performing a dual role as risk facilitator and a member of the management team for the work. In this situation you may well be a risk owner for some risks, in addition to being the facilitator for others.

Probability is hard to calculate

Not just hard – impossible in many situations. Unless you have comprehensive historical data that is directly relevant to the risk (which is rare), then all you can do is guess how likely it is that the risk will occur. Start with whether the group judges the risk to be more or less likely to occur, then decide how much more than 50 per cent or how much less than 50 per cent feels right. Most companies have standard probability scales that force the assessment of probability into a small number of ranges, for example, very high probability is greater than 70 per cent chance. Risk management standards judge this to be best practice.

We are poor at prioritisation and get bogged down at this point

People most commonly prioritise risks by using a combination of probability (what's the chance this risk event will happen) and impact (how much it matters if it does). Where risk management standards advise using company standard probability scales as mentioned above, they state that work specific impact scales should be created. Our advice on how to do this is as follows:

- Think about what objectives matter most to your work
- Define what would be a catastrophic impact on each objective, for example, what time delay would be a 'showstopper'
- Define what impact would be insignificant, for example, the amount of money that it is not worth proactively trying to save
- Define impact scales (three, four, or five categories) that represent the specific impact on objectives that would really matter to your work
- If you invest time in doing this, that is, defining how you will prioritise before you start, it will save you hours of frustration later.

We do a reasonable job at prioritisation, but then ignore low priority risks

As we have pointed out in Chapter 6, it is really important that the facilitator helps the group focus on the highest priority risks at each workshop. But the risk prioritisation is only a snapshot in time. Who's to say that the assessment of probability and impact will be the same in a month's time? The risk owner is the person who should keep an eye on this, but as facilitator you may need to play an active role to ensure this happens. It might be necessary at some point to hold a special session to readdress those lower priority risks and see what can be learned.

We need to use appropriate ways to respond to risk – not just mitigate!

There are many different ways to respond to risks. The option you choose will depend on a number of things, including the appetite for risk (how much uncertainty can you tolerate) and the resources available (does it make sense to invest time and money now to reduce the uncertainty). Chapter 2 has a whole section on responding to risks, outlining all the options you can choose. Why not use the guidance in the response planning section of Chapter 5 with your group and overtly consider options other than mitigation, which is only relevant to reducing a bad risk. Changing language often leads to a change in thinking that is very beneficial for the overall process.

Out of the frying pan, into the fire: we always seem to forget about the secondary risk

Identification of secondary risks is a part of response planning. Make sure your process makes this crystal clear and that risk owners understand their responsibilities. A response plan is not complete without secondary risks identified and described well in the risk register. We find also that when you make this a discipline you get a much better quality of risk response in the first place because all the consequences are thought through.

People tend not to follow up on the risk plan

Why have a separate risk plan if actions don't happen? Add the risk actions into the project, programme, or operational plan so you can be sure they are resourced and monitored. You also need to find ways of holding risk owners accountable. There are ideas to help you in Chapter 5.

We often leave workshops with poor outcomes: inappropriate actions, no agreed plan to manage, or both

Come to an agreement about outcomes of your workshop at the start, using the start-up process outlined in Chapter 6. Challenge actions if you feel they are inappropriate. It is also important to check people's intent to carry out their specific risk response actions. Put in place some sort of follow-up mechanism.

We leave workshops with plans, then behave as if the risk has already been managed

A while ago, Ruth was speaking with a colleague who is a very experienced risk consultant. During the conversation it became apparent that even experienced people can be fooled into thinking that a plan to respond to a risk is a 'done deal'. Of course, a plan to respond is just that. It needs to be resourced and implemented if the exposure to risk is to be changed. The example we were discussing involved eliminating the cause of a threat. It would be normal to say the residual risk was zero in this situation, but of course this is only true *if* the response plan has been successfully implemented. Facilitators need to be very clear with their language and talk about the risk remaining should the plan be unsuccessful. We also need good systems for tracking and monitoring the success of response actions. If we leave out this step, we are only doing risk assessment, not managing risks properly.

We handle risks by listing problems and, all too often, random thoughts

By raising this as a problem, you know that this isn't too useful. Look at Chapter 5 to gain a fuller understanding of the steps you need to cover along with the process that you can follow and adapt to suit your organisation. But don't lose those inputs, just turn them into good risk descriptions later. People are likely to be grateful that their thoughts have been listened to and channelled into a useful process.

I'm a business analyst, working with requirements. We don't have any traceability of risks to requirements. This can cause problems with changes of scope.

Add in traceability if that will help your work. When considering risks to requirements, you could hold a separate workshop. During this workshop you could link each risk to the appropriate requirement.

Pitfalls when facilitating

You can find advice about facilitation, both in and out of workshops in Chapter 4, Chapter 6, and Chapter 7. In this section, you'll find some quick tips about avoiding pitfalls in the future when you are facilitating.

I don't know how it happens, but whenever I work with groups I always seem to end up with the actions. What can I do?

This is fundamental to risk facilitation. Risks are uncertainties that matter to the group's objectives, not yours. This is something you need to reflect throughout the risk process. Remind the group that you are there to make their process easy but that they own the risks. There are lots of tips on how to do this in Chapter 4, Chapters 5, and Chapter 6.

Too often, we 'do' risk at the start, then 'it's done' so we leave it alone and the process dies

Don't worry, you are not alone! Avoiding this is the main point of risk facilitation. We've found many organisations where risk is 'done' at the start for compliance reasons and then abandoned once the boxes are ticked. This is a waste of time and money. Having said that, can you adapt the tick boxes into action steps and use these with other tools to form part of your risk process?

We recommend that you develop your skills as a risk facilitator, particularly focusing on engaging people and energising the risk process to keep it alive.

My organisation has no concept of risk facilitation

Risk facilitation is a new skill that is becoming more important as organisations take on increasing amounts of change and more risky new ventures. Even facilitation is a fairly new profession that is developing rapidly, as is risk management. By combining the two, you're becoming a pioneer, likely to add much value over the years ahead.

Remember too, that to become a really effective risk facilitator, you will need to change the culture of your organisation, particularly their attitude toward risk management. See Vivien, Chris, and Anna's stories in Chapter 4 for inspiration on how to turn this from 'boring and necessary' to 'beneficial and essential'.

Some of our risk facilitators get far too involved

It is quite common for the manager to attempt to be the risk facilitator for their own work. The trouble here is that the manager is then tied up facilitating the workshop, rather than giving their unique view on the risks. Worse still, in this situation the facilitator may only give airtime to views that support their own. We recommend the use of an independent facilitator. This person could be another manager on an exchange from another part of the organisation, for example a project management office, or could be an external consultant. Remember that they need to understand both risk and facilitation, as well as being experienced in running risk workshops (see the hamburger model – with the lettuce and tomato in Chapter 4).

We have people who are meant to manage risk, but they are incompetent as facilitators

This book has explained why facilitation is essential to making risk management work. Can these risk managers become good facilitators with support and training? If not, you may need to change the way your organisation manages risk or bring in new people with the appropriate skills in both risk *and* facilitation.

I have been doing risk facilitation for years, sometimes making it up as I go along. How can I take what I've learned from this book and develop my skills further, as well as adding some theoretical underpinning of what I already know?

As we've said before, facilitation is a fairly new skill and its application to risk management is even newer. Congratulations for developing your skills and competence through years of practice and learning lessons as you go.

To develop a theoretical underpinning of what you already know, and build on the contents of this book, you could join a risk facilitation course. Look for ones that combine expertise in risk and facilitation, enabling you to learn from both disciplines at the same time.

The alternative is to join a general facilitation course, although this will not cover the subtle and specialist areas of risk management. For more information on risk facilitation training, contact the authors or sign up at www.makingriskwork.com.

People don't understand the point of the workshop

This is fundamental. Everything else flows from this. You need to be really clear about the purpose of the workshop, both in the preparation phase and throughout the session itself. Successful workshops can flow from an agreed purpose. Confusion about the purpose almost always results in poor outcomes.

We tend to lack clear objectives when I attend risk workshops

The facilitator needs to set up and agree clear objectives, as well as the time plan, roles, ground rules, and what happens next, at the start of each meeting.

Poor facilitation hinders our workshops

It happens! You can learn facilitation from risk facilitation experts like us or alternatively bring in experienced facilitators to run some of your risk workshops. Watching experienced facilitators is one way that people learn that good facilitation is crucial to making the risk management process work.

We usually have the wrong people in the workshop, either some are missing or too many attend. Often, it's hard to get the right people to turn up.

People are much more likely to attend if they know the session will be interesting and worthwhile. As previously mentioned, it's important to be really clear about the point of your risk workshop, in particular which steps of the risk management process you plan to address. If you do this, it should be easier to work out who needs to be there and who doesn't. It's much easier to convince people that they are needed (or not!) if you have a clear purpose and objectives for each workshop.

In order to get the right people to attend, you need to convince them of the benefits of the workshop and why they need to be there. This may require one-to-one conversations with key people prior to your workshop to convince them.

Another way to make it more likely that people will attend is to ask for their input about which date suits them best. If you've done this, it is harder for them to refuse to come if you hold the workshop on a date they've already agreed with.

Once you have people in the room, or together via technology, you can engage their interest and enthusiasm by running a very effective and enjoyable workshop using the tips in Chapter 6, plus Chapter 7 if virtual. Risk workshops have all too often been seen as boring, and once this belief is shattered you should find it less of a challenge to get people to attend.

In our workshops the organisational culture and politics are often not understood, and this causes problems

It is normal for workshops to bring people together from different parts of an organisation. Not only that, but sometimes there will be people from other organisations present, for example a client, key supplier, partner, or regulator. It is therefore quite normal for people to have different goals, styles, and ways of working. The more you prepare in advance the better. Try to find out as much as you can about the workshop participants so you can plan your approach accordingly. The more you, as facilitator, understand about organisational culture, the more you can anticipate and respond to problems if they arise. You are ideally placed to treat everyone with equal respect. When you do this, you may well find that everyone else follows your example. Your role is to make sure everyone can contribute despite the organisational culture and politics.

It seems that we are too close to the detail when we come up with risks; we don't have a holistic view

There are a few ways that facilitators can help here. One is by focusing the team on what matters, that is, the objectives. While some of these will be detailed, there will be other, more holistic objectives, that need attention too. Another way that a facilitator can help is by using prompt lists to help people think across all areas. A generic example would be to use the PESTLE prompt (Political, Economical, Sociological, Technological, Legal, Environmental). There are many other ways to structure prompt lists to help the team think broadly, as well as deeply.

We tend to go off track and lose focus

Keep the purpose of your workshop at the front of everybody's mind by writing it up on the wall or placing it on a shared screen. It is the facilitator's main role to keep people 'on purpose' and to flag up when the group drifts off track. One way of doing this in an in-person meeting is to give each person two cards – one red and the other one yellow. Using a football referee analogy, explain at the start of the meeting that they can wave a yellow card if the meeting starts to go off track. This is usually enough to bring people back to the point with a smile! Using this method our experience is that red cards, signifying a major issue, are seldom required.

We get overwhelmed by detail

There can be a lot of detail in a risk workshop. Make sure the big picture and benefits are visible to all throughout the workshop. Also, you should keep to an appropriate level of detail for the audience. You may also find that you are simply trying to do too much in one workshop. Chapter 5 provides some tips about splitting up the risk process and using a combination of workshops and work outside of such sessions.

We can't seem to identify risks

Risks aren't always easy to find, are they? Go through the process outlined in Chapter 5. Start with causes – things happening now – that can stimulate thought. Make sure that you have a wide range of people involved so that all areas are covered. Use creativity to help people to come up with a range of ideas.

Why do I need to care about risk attitude?

In short, risk attitude is important because ignoring it will mean that human perspectives are unmanaged, potentially leading to poor-quality decision-making. Risk attitude is used to describe a person's chosen response to a risk. Risk attitude is personal, situational, and driven by perceptions. This means that your risk attitudes vary from time to time. Groups can also hold risk attitudes. Again, you should expect these also to vary from time to time, depending on the situational and other factors that influence perception (see Chapter 3).

Risk attitude is normally expressed by using labels such as:

- *Risk averse* meaning that the person would choose to act in order to increase certainty
- *Risk seeking* meaning that the person would be comfortable with the uncertainty without doing anything to reduce it.

Other labels commonly used are risk tolerant and risk neutral. See Chapter 2 for more details. Risk attitude is a massive subject, although you can gain a good grasp fairly quickly if you want to. A good place to start is www.making-decisions.com.

People tell me not to bother with bias and just get on with the work

Sometimes the people who tell you that are correct. We can reasonably ignore biases if the decision doesn't matter that much. When decisions do matter – when they are risky and important – it makes the decision even more risky if we ignore bias. All people are biased by a whole range of things and how we are biased is not immediately obvious to us (that's the point – if we were totally aware, we would fix it). We can't eliminate bias, but we can be more aware and make sure through our facilitation of risk that we don't walk blindly into poor decisions.

People I work with are very risk averse

We need to be careful about labelling whole groups of people in this way. It may well be that the prevailing culture of your organisation is to minimise uncertainty as far as possible and to feel uncomfortable if there are unmanaged risks about – that's what risk averse means – but that doesn't mean that it's useful to assume that all people will always behave like that. In a typical working team, there will be a whole range of risk attitudes 'in the room'. A crucial skill of the facilitator is to be aware of your own attitude to risk at that time and to be able to spot decision-biases that may be arising from inappropriate risk attitudes. Sometimes it's good just to name what you see and bring the risk attitude or bias to the attention of the group so you can help them explore what's going on. It also helps to be clear about risk appetite and what tolerance for risk the organisation has – see Chapter 2 for more on this.

Too often, we have powerful people in the room, and they tend to sway or block risk. Senior people influence or sometimes even direct discussion. How can we deal with this?

Make sure that you are aware of any senior (or very junior) people who might cause hierarchy to be an issue within your workshop. You might need to plan a range of processes to keep the workshop on track. In some circumstances, it makes sense to discuss this issue with the attendees individually, explaining that in order to assess risks properly everyone's input is needed. It can be useful to design the process for anonymous input (either before or during the workshop) or to split into small groups and then present back as a group, rather than individually.

Some people are naturally dominant and talk over others

Yes, they are. If you have someone who is speaking much more than everyone else, it will affect your workshop. Find out if this is likely, given past experiences, and plan accordingly. During the workshop, there are several ways to deal with this. The easiest is calling a break and talking to the individual concerned. Often, just pointing out to the group as a whole that one person has been speaking for 10 minutes and asking what they'd like to do about this can do the trick. It may be that they are happy to hear more from him or her. This solution also has the added bonus of leaving the ownership of the problem with the group, rather than trying to solve it yourself.

Key people keep quiet in my workshops

Prepare beforehand for the range of people who will be in your workshop. If you know that some people are unlikely to speak up, then you can plan different ways to obtain their input. As with the previous pitfall, anonymous input can be useful, such as writing on sticky notes or breaking into small groups for discussion and then reporting back. If your quiet people are happy to speak out to the whole group as long as they are not interrupted, then you could use the 'talking stick' approach. In this approach you choose an object to act as a 'talking stick' and set a rule that the only person allowed to speak is the one holding the stick or who has been allocated it virtually.

Groups I lead often spend too long concentrating on the 'wrong' risks, for example those with low probability and low impact

It's true that low probability, low impact risks are not the top priority – but that doesn't mean they can be ignored. Each one of those will have a risk owner who is hopefully keeping an eye on the risky situation. Nevertheless, your job as a risk facilitator is to help the group use their time to best effect, so you can challenge people if they are clearly not focusing on the priority matters. Remember also what we've said in Chapter 5 about not doing everything in workshops. Risk response planning is something that can be done by the risk owner once all the risks to objectives have been identified and prioritised.

I don't get honest answers when I ask people about risks

That's interesting. What do you mean by an honest answer? It sounds as if there is some background work for you to do as a facilitator before your workshops, and you need to talk with the individuals involved. Is it just a different viewpoint? What are the political issues involved?

What about vested interests?

We all have vested interests. People in your workshops will come from a variety of areas and of course they will have their own interests at heart. It is your job as a facilitator to help the group to find a way of working through any challenges.

People keep inventing inapplicable or unrealistic risks

If you are using techniques such as brainstorming, then it is natural that some inapplicable risks will be raised because we want people to open up and be creative. At this stage, quantity is more important than quality. But quality needs to follow as the initial brainstorm is turned into well-described risks. Only at this consolidation point should points be removed if they are not uncertainties that would matter if they occurred. Of course, it really helps if you are very clear about the objectives and impact areas that matter the most before starting to identify risks. It can also help to use risk categories to achieve this same purpose.

We need more than one workshop, but it is so hard to engage people and retain their commitment. What should we do?

It is usual to need more than one workshop. In fact, we would strongly urge that risk management work takes place over a series of activities, only some of which are workshops. Resist the pressure to cram all of the risk work into one marathon session. Your challenge is to engage people. A series of much shorter, but effective, risk workshops might well do the trick, especially if they are tightly focused and fun to participate in.

It's a challenge to maintain regular attendance at risk workshops

We'd suggest that the first step is to make sure that you really need the same people at each session. Do these sessions have a clear reason to exist other than the fact that it is a particular time of the month? You may well find that each workshop needs a slightly different set of participants. If the same people are needed each time, perhaps you could vary the format of the workshop, trying new techniques to achieve the same objectives. If you can keep the sessions interesting, people are more likely to make them a priority. Have a look at the case studies in Chapter 3, where Vivien, Chris, and Anna achieved this. Of course, there may be times when people want to attend, but cannot. Then you need to think about how you can include them by running a hybrid meeting, as in Chapter 7.

We can't meet in person to run a risk workshop as we're spread out geographically (or there is a pandemic, or whatever . . .)

Run your workshop virtually using technology. We suggest using collaboration tools with shared whiteboards to make things visual for all participants. These workshops need facilitators who are comfortable with facilitating risk plus facilitating virtually. For all that this entails, see Chapter 7. Good virtual workshops are not just about having access to the right technology, although this helps enormously. Skilled virtual facilitation will keep everyone engaged throughout the workshop.

In hybrid risk workshops, those in the room go off on their own, leaving the remote people out of the discussion

This happens. It's so easy for those in the room together to pick up on the nuances of conversation and just carry on, forgetting about those who are joining by technology. It's not a level playing field, and the facilitator needs to do all they can to level the playing field. Set up how you'll work together and how you'll include the remote participants right at the start. This could include choosing to be #remotefirst and calling on remote people for input before asking anyone in the room. There is much more you can do in Chapter 7.

I'm terrified of destructive confrontation at my workshop

If you think this is likely you need to take even more care to follow good practice. Set up ground rules in advance, agreeing 'How we work together', before any confrontation happens. Facilitate any conflict carefully. Always remain open to task and process conflict, that is, where people have different viewpoints based on their role and experience. Make sure everyone who needs to has an opportunity to have their say. This is necessary for good decision-making.

Relationship conflict is another matter. Address this as soon as you can, as it can be very destructive. There are ideas on how to do this in Chapter 6.

Our workshops contain so many different cultural perspectives, tolerances, and attitudes to risk. How can we cope?

First of all, acknowledge that this is normal. As part of your stakeholder analysis, you need to find out as much as possible about the participants who will attend. This will help you plan sessions that respect cultural differences and get the best out of people. Of course, you will learn a lot more within a session if you are able to remain 'present' and open to the people. There are some helpful hints how to do this in Chapter 6.

Sometimes people in workshops seem to fear identifying risks, as if by mentioning them, they're making the risk more likely – why?

Although it may sound silly to suggest that simply mentioning a risk might 'tempt fate' and make it more likely, we know that some people have this view. The reality is that the reverse happens. Articulating a risk opens up our senses to think what we might do about it. We can't actively respond to every risk, but we can be mindful, with our 'radar' tuned in. Facilitators should put effort into ensuring they create as safe a place as possible for risk identification so that the process is as creative and divergent as you can make it. The risks that individuals think about, but don't share, may well be the very ones that actually occur.

People use jargon or technical language that half the group don't understand

As a risk facilitator, you will need to make sure that any jargon or technical language is translated so that everyone can understand. People don't like to own up to not understanding jargon though, so you will need to ask simple questions such as 'What do you mean by that three-letter abbreviation?' You'll find that many others in your workshop will be thinking the same thing but are reluctant to ask such 'dumb questions'. In reality these are intelligent questions that need asking. As facilitator, you need to be brave. Others will respect you for making things clear.

We always seem to run out of time

This is a perennial problem, with poor facilitation at the root. Be clear from the start what your purpose and objectives are for a session. Arrange multiple, shorter workshops rather than trying to get everything done in one go. Design a clear time plan with realistic amounts of time for each part. An experienced facilitator can help here, even if they're only available in the design phase. Appoint a timekeeper.

We don't have enough time to reach a consensus

Is true consensus really necessary for your group? If so, you need to plan in enough time to get there. If not, stop once you have what you need.

What risk workshop? In our organisation, risk workshops are not an accepted way of dealing with risk as you're expected to work on this alone.

Explain that effective risk management relies on having a variety of different perspectives from stakeholders to gain a full picture of the risks that are perceived to exist. By working on risk management on your own, you're likely to miss out many important risks. Another benefit of workshops is that a great deal of information can be analysed by the group in a much shorter time than if you were to go and talk to each stakeholder in turn. You can gain instant feedback, too. Having said all that, it is important to remember that not all the steps in the risk management process are best suited to workshops (see Chapter 5).

People don't understand why we need a workshop at all

Explain the purpose of the workshop before convening the group. Make sure that the people involved understand what each session needs to achieve and what their role in the workshop will be. Add in the benefits of risk workshops and how much value they can add.

Our workshops are not tailored correctly

Well, now's a good time to get going. As a risk facilitator, you need to adapt to suit the different cultures (profession, countries, and organisations) and needs of all of the participants involved.

In our organisation, risks are not published and shared. There is a lot of secrecy involved.

Is there a good reason for the secrecy? Challenge this if not. You may need to adapt the workshop to allow for the right levels of confidentiality.

Our workshops are scuppered by hidden agendas and politics

Prepare well and ask stakeholders about the possible impact of politics and hidden agendas beforehand. Set up and agree ground rules: 'How we work together'. If you assume good intent from everyone, you'll be more likely to get it. If you wouldn't describe yourself as politically savvy, make sure that there are others in the room who are able to help you to be effective, despite politics. Ensure you have a senior sponsor to start off your workshop and, if appropriate, to remain throughout.

Risk workshops are boring and seen as uncreative

We've shared lots of ideas to overcome this throughout this book. We encourage you to try some of them and to let us know how you get along. There is lots of additional help that can be provided once you have some experience of the fundamentals we have explained.

Pitfalls when trying to create a culture where risk management works well

Reactive heroes, not proactive risk managers, are valued in my organisation

We often hear people say this. Fortunately, we hear this from senior leaders as much as from their staff, and this is positive as we detect a real desire to change. Leaders, at all levels, have to take responsibility for making the change. It can really help to set personal objectives for all staff that encourage proactive and anticipatory behaviours. Our experience is that the culture starts to change when money spent on actual problems (issues) is tracked *and* there is a focus on learning lessons from completed work. Most importantly, everyone needs to 'walk the talk', that is, make it a daily habit to discuss what's risky and why.

We're so busy doing day-to-day delivery that risk management gets squeezed out

Yes, but how much of your day-to-day delivery is caused by managing actual problems and firefighting? Many of your current issues would once have been uncertain threats, which could have been managed proactively. What about your missed opportunities? Until you put an appropriate risk management process into place, you'll continue to be affected by avoidable issues and missed opportunities. Unfortunately, to see an improvement, you need to put in additional effort in the short term. This quickly repays as you start to manage risks and so there are fewer crises.

No one can see the pain we're avoiding. We're not noticing the improvements we make.

This is a tricky one. Of course, the work that you do to avoid costly threats is valuable. But to convince others of the value of your work, you will need to measure it in some way. See Chapter 2 for ideas on what to measure.

Senior managers in my organisation don't buy in to risk. They can't see the value. It's seen as a waste of time and counterproductive.

This is another area where measures can help. The baseline metrics of 'how it is now' can be an eye-opener for senior managers who may not have paid much attention to the detail of risk management. To build support, you need to be able to explain – or better still – show the benefits of risk management to people in your organisation at all levels. See the case studies in Chapter 3 to see how Vivien, Chris, and Anna were influential in their respective organisations. This may involve learning lessons from past failures in managing risk. Offering appropriate training can help spread the understanding across your organisation. The key thing though is to focus on what matters most and make progress visible.

My organisation tends to 'jump on' anyone who comes up with negative threats. How can I bring in good risk management practices without limiting my career?

The most effective environment for risk management is one where there is a 'no blame' culture. In such a culture, people are rewarded for highlighting threats that can then dealt with appropriately in advance of any negative impact. Think about how you can encourage this. Sometimes it's useful to talk about a possible response to a threat when you first mention it. Doing this is often perceived as positive, that is 'this bad thing may happen, but we can do this now . . .' Raising the risk only, with no potential solution, can be seen as negative. In our experience though, negative reactions to risk identification from senior management can often happen when risk registers are full of 'normal' risk, such as statements like 'we may not have the resources when we need them'. This is not useful. General variability about resource availability needs to be built into plans. Specific risks associated with specific resources for specific work are useful to include in the risk register only if the resource type is scarce and the work is critical.

When we present the results of our workshops, senior managers think we're being negative. They say things like: 'I want a can-do attitude – solutions not problems'.

It's important to make sure that the senior managers understand the benefits of good risk management. Once that's in place, then make sure you present both positive opportunities as well as the negative threats. Be careful to present these at an appropriate level of detail for the people you're presenting to. With senior managers, this can be much more 'big picture' than you might be used to as a risk practitioner.

Our organisation lacks deep experience in risk and in risk facilitation. How can we develop this quickly?

While this book has a detailed plan for doing risk management, it can take some time to build up from scratch. You can speed this up by bringing in risk facilitation experts like us to support you while your organisation is developing. Do get in touch with the authors if you feel this might be useful. With help, people can develop the skills they need for your organisation to become self-sufficient in implementing effective risk management.

This chapter has discussed many pitfalls, all raised by existing risk practitioners. You may be feeling a little overwhelmed with all the detail. We'll therefore finish this book with a quick summary – our 'Ten golden guidelines for the risk facilitator'.

9 Ten golden guidelines for the risk facilitator

This final chapter is deliberately very short. It summarises the book with ten golden guidelines for anyone involved in making risk management work through risk facilitation.

1 There are lots of pitfalls, but you can plan and prepare carefully and avoid falling into them.

2 Risk management is difficult to do well, and a facilitator can make a big difference. The role of the facilitator is to make it easy.

DOI: 10.4324/9781003245858-9

152 Ten golden guidelines for the risk facilitator

3 Risk facilitators need a whole range of personal qualities, as well as a deep understanding of the risk management process.

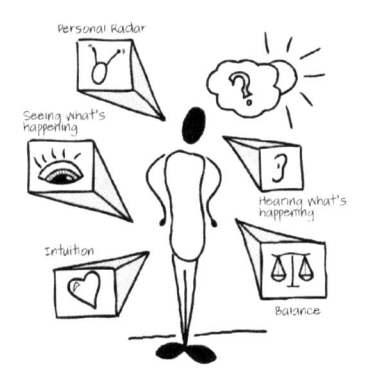

4 Risk facilitators also need to be 'vegetarian'. They focus on the facilitation process and the risk management process but stay out of the 'meat' of the work content.

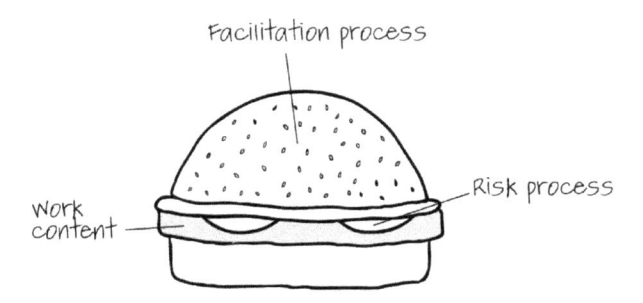

5 Risk facilitators need to engage the right people at all times.

6 Risk facilitators need to keep groups energised, as well as engaged, while maintaining their own level of energy, whether their workshops are in person, hybrid, or fully remote.

7 Risk facilitators add lots of value when they have the skills and credibility to challenge the participants. They need to resist the temptation to challenge on content, staying vegetarian.

8 Careful preparation is the key to successful workshops.

9 Things do go wrong. Different people have different perceptions of what is risky and why. Conflicts will arise. Stay calm and help the group to find a way through.

10 Facilitate risk management well, and you'll engage others and make sure that the risk register is cobweb free!

Risk management is very important if organisations are to make good decisions in risky and important situations. As a risk facilitator, you can add real value by making the process easy for your colleagues, so they can be creative, productive, and have fun.

Index

alien invasion 85

bias 3, 33, 89, 97, 105, 116, 138; cognitive 37–40; heuristic 35–37

conflict 49–50, 86–87, 99, 143
conscious awareness 43–44

decisions 1, 17, 27, 31–32, 45, 69, 82, 88, 138

facilitation 47–64; confidentiality 87; consensus 83, 118, 145; diverse 48, 62; ground rules 87, 93; hidden agendas 88, 146; hierarchy 48, 139; jargon 144; lessons learned 95, 100; open, honest 140; preparation 106, 134; recorder (scribe) 87, 92; staying calm 94–95; timekeeper 87, 92, 144–145; vested interests 141

governance 8, 11, 26, 69

hamburger analogy 52
hybrid 70, 103–120, 142

independent input. 43–44, 89
issues, confusion with risks 12, 51, 57, 68, 91, 124

Magic 6™ 92, 115

organisational culture and politics 54, 64, 135–136

pitfalls: with applying the risk management process 122–130; when creating a culture where risk management works well 147–150; when facilitating 131–146

reframing 43–44, 89
remote 3, 49, 70–71, 103–120
risk: appetite 13, 128, 136; attitude 17–20; capacity 13; descriptions 14; log, register 16, 25–26, 72, 76, 78–80, 100–101, 122; opportunities/upsides 9–10, 20, 25–26, 70–72, 126, 147, 149; perception, triple strand of influences 18, 32–33, 42; risk averse 20; risk neutral 20; risk seeking 20; risk tolerant 20; secondary risk 25, 76, 129; threats/downsides 9–10, 20, 25–26, 70–72, 126, 147, 149; tolerance 13, 69
risk facilitator 47–48, 51–53, 62–63, 86–87, 105, 152–154; case studies 55–62; development path 62–64; skills 48–50, 62–64
risk management: benefits, measures 27; culture 56–59, 69, 147–148; standards 20–23
risk management process 65–82; actions, intentionality 100; assessment 12–15; chance 8, 15; consequence, impact, effect on objectives 8, 15–16; describe (cause-risk event-impact) 14–15; identify 70–72; initiate, risk management plan 69–70; keeping it alive 25–26, 78–81; plan B, contingent, fallback, real options 23; prioritise 72–74, 127–129; response 21, 76–78, 128–129

risk owner/ownership 21–22, 80, 127–129

team development 98

virtual 49–50, 103–119, 142; definition 104; leadership 106–109

workshops 83–102, 109–116; anonymous input 50, 96–97; boring 66, 146; environment 90, 112; hybrid 105–106, 110–111, 113–115; going wrong 95, 154; in-person 70, 73–74, 83–102, 136; keeping people engaged 93–94, 110–111, 136; more than one 96, 141; objectives 86, 92; participants 88–90; preparation 22, 85–91; purpose 85–86, 90, 115, 134–135; remote 103–106, 111–113; virtual 109–116

Milton Keynes UK
Ingram Content Group UK Ltd.
UKHW021011270924
448921UK00006B/34

9 781032 158358